A PLACE NOT A PLACE

Reflection and Possibility in Museums and Libraries

DAVID CARR

ROWMAN & LITTLEFIELD PUBLISHERS, INC.
Lanham • New York • Toronto • Oxford

ALTAMIRA PRESS

A division of Rowman & Littlefield Publishers, Inc.
A wholly owned subsidiary of The Rowman & Littlefield Publishing Group, Inc.
4501 Forbes Boulevard, Suite 200
Lanham, MD 20706
www.altamirapress.com

PO Box 317
Oxford
OX2 9RU, UK

Copyright © 2006 by David Carr

All rights reserved. No part of this publication may be reproduced, stored
in a retrieval system, or transmitted in any form or by any means, electronic,
mechanical, photocopying, recording, or otherwise, without the prior permission
of the publisher.

British Library Cataloguing in Publication Information Available

Library of Congress Cataloguing-in-Publication Data

Carr, David, 1945–
  A place not a place: reflection and possibility in museums and libraries / David
Carr.
    p. cm.
  Includes bibliographical references (p.) and index.
  ISBN-13: 978-0-7591-1019-9 (cloth : alk. paper)
  ISBN-10: 0-7591-1019-0 (cloth : alk. paper)
  ISBN-13: 978-0-7591-1020-5 (pbk. : alk. paper)
  ISBN-10: 0-7591-1020-4 (pbk. : alk. paper)
  1. United States—Cultural policy. 2. United States—Intellectual life.
3. Libraries—Social aspects—United States. 4. Museums—Social aspects—
United States. 5. Learning and scholarship—Social aspects—United States.
6. Politics and culture—United States. 7. Art and state—United States. I. Title.

E169.12.C2785 2006
  306.0973—dc22   2006003327

Printed in the United States of America

♾™ The paper used in this publication meets the minimum requirements of
American National Standard for Information Sciences—Permanence of Paper for
Printed Library Materials, ANSI/NISO Z39.48-1992.

CONTENTS

ACKNOWLEDGMENTS

"The Cognitive Management of Cultural Institutions," originally published under the title "Minds in Museums and Libraries: The Cognitive Management of Cultural Institutions," in *Teachers College Record*, Fall 1991, is reprinted with the permission of Blackwell Publishing.

"What I Saw in the Museum," is reprinted with permission from *Museum News*, September/October 2004. Copyright 2004, the American Association of Museums. All rights reserved.

Two essays, originally published in *Curator* under slightly different titles, "Five Thoughtful Exercises" (42, no. 2) and "Observing Collaboration" (48, no. 3), are reprinted with the permission of Rowman & Littlefield Publishing Group, Inc.

"Reading Beyond the Museum" and a section of "Memory" previously titled "The Personal Past in Public Space" were originally published in *Journal of Museum Education*. Reprinted with permission of Museum Education Roundtable, all rights reserved. For more information contact: Museum Education Roundtable, 621 Pennsylvania Ave. SE, Washington, D.C., 20003 or go online to www.mer-online.org or contact them by e-mail at info@mer-online.org.

A different section of "Memory" was presented originally as a keynote address to the Council of American Jewish Museums, and subsequently published in an edited form in its newsletter. Reprinted with permission of the Council of American Jewish Museums.

"What I Read in the Library" was originally presented as "In Celebration of Library and Community in Bainbridge, Georgia." Southwest Georgia Regional Library System, 2002, National Library Award Community Celebration, Gilbert H. Gragg Library, Bainbridge, Georgia, January 21, 2003. The author is grateful for the invitation to speak that day.

Other parts of this collection were originally presented at these places: the Howe Library, Hanover, New Hampshire, February 2003; the Trustees of Old Sturbridge Village, Sturbridge, Massachusetts, October 2003; the History Section of the North Carolina Museums Association, March 2004; the Museums Association of New York, April 2004; the Nantucket Historical Association, July 2004; the Mid-Atlantic Museum Association, October 2004; St. Mary's College of Maryland, October 2004; Louisiana State University Libraries, November 2004; the North Carolina Museum of Art, January 2005; Arizona State Library, March 2005; Florida State Library Association, April 2005; and the Southeast Museums Conference, October 2005.

REFLECTIVE USERS:
AN INTRODUCTION

We are learners. We build. We observe. We reflect. We experiment. We explore. We fail. We follow. We diverge. We generate. We express. We feel. We play. We imagine. We speak. We dream. We participate in the engaging flow of experience, and we prepare ourselves to ask questions when our thoughts are under siege by doubt. This is how we grow into our own lives, how we take up our work as agents and designers in our own course of becoming stronger. How are we learners? We endure and we trust, we look, we want, we move forward toward something we cannot clearly see.

We want a situation where the dimensions of our experiences are often unclear to us until the moment they happen. We want that freshness and unfamiliarity; we hope to be surprised. We want a situation where there are many different kinds of things we do not yet understand, so we can select from among them, and everywhere we turn we will think hypothetically, tentatively, keeping our thoughts open as long as we possibly can. We want a place where knowing and thinking restore our senses of a purposeful future and remind us of what might await us; as we move forward we want to be stimulated by what others know and think about, and how they live their lives.

Situations of this kind, where our experiences are fresh, vivid, and sustained over time—situations where we observe in common with other people and engage in new language to describe what we experience—prepare us to know ideas and concepts we will encounter elsewhere in our lives. More than twenty years ago, in *Frames of Mind*, Howard Gardner wrote that experiences of particular kinds prepare us for new knowledge and the information we derive from new situations.[1] Reasoning analogically from the widely known concept of "at risk" populations, Gardner described certain people as "'at promise' for the flowering of certain talent."[2] More than twenty years later, how and where do we assist people who are "at prom-ise" to reveal themselves and extend their abilities to think and become, and how do we come to understand and foster their experiences? How do we make the recognition of such promise more widespread?

If we care to answer that question, it will happen one reflective user at a time, one thinking person at a time. One at a time: the process of think-ing and the awakening of promise change by moments. The promise of cul-tural institutions lies in their openness for our exploration as places for learning and thinking differently. When we go to them our experiences are about the present, about our own lived experiences as they happen. Yet our momentary experiences are also about the slow unfolding of our thoughts and memories. When we speak our questions to a librarian or walk with a companion through museum galleries, we are communicating to each other face to face, not over a distance or through a device. We are encouraged to think for ourselves, as individuals do, and to experience that independence and courage as a matter of course. We are free to place our attention any-where, to pause, to return, to move away, to stay. When we use a library or a museum, every experience affects the next experience. When we speak to each other, our words become parts of our lived experiences of each other. We need not make our thinking small, correct, or purposeful. We need not act as anyone other than ourselves, and yet it is not always useful to act in the interests of ourselves alone. We are participants in our culture, of our culture. We are free to think of the known and of unknowns as well. We are able to feel unafraid of change.

Change requires caution; it means that we lengthen the tether that moors us to the familiar. But it also means cultivating an openness to po-tentially extraordinary experiences, remarkable things to see and grasp. In an essay titled "Courage and Cognitive Growth in Children and Scientists," Howard Gruber wrote about the motions of children's minds.

> We would probably discover, if we looked a little more closely at those moments when the child's thinking really seems to move, that the child experiences a sense of exhilaration. When we speak of "insight" or the "Aha experience," it is not just seeing something new. It is feeling. And what the person is feeling is both the promise and the threat of this un-known that is just opening up. When we think new thoughts we really are changing our relations with the world around us, including our so-cial moorings. . . .[3]
>
> A large change in thought really involves abandoning a paradigm—in other words, abandoning a whole way of thought: a group of ideas, methods, sources of evidence, relationships with colleagues, and so on.

> Since this change cannot take place instantaneously, every change made in an individual's way of thought moves him away from his own past.[4]

We are all "at promise" in this way, able to live up to our own selves. No longer a child, I find myself in these ideas. I am surprised to recognize as a personal truth that learning is my way of moving away from my own past, and that this is the single strand most important to my well-being: constructing a self that moves forward on intellect and trust, and away from a childish past.

But I have also come to understand that moving forward most likely happens for us alone; when we learn, we are apart from classes and schools, even when we are within them. Or we are perhaps with another person, not a stranger, with whom we hold in common those two energies, intellect and trust. When we explore ideas in dialogue, I think that we come closer to the way that learning happens. I find that there is no situation of depth for learning over a lifetime without the presence (real or imagined) of another human being breathing strength and character into it. We sometimes need teachers, but we must leave them, and carry their lessons away to relationships beyond teaching.

Though our spirits may expand and strengthen in solitude, I believe that all useful learning requires a place for its expression or construction. There is no tool without its user, outcome without its process, thought without a context, because cognitive motion of the kind that Gruber describes always implies the effects of the tool, the outcome of the act, or the resonance of the thought. In this way, we "are changing our relations with the world." But we require a place of change; for me, changes have the permanent association of place, and presence, situation, and event.

Knowledge has no purpose or place without having its interpreters, artists, and communicators. They hold, transform, and transmit knowledge; their minds construct a shared, working worldview of practices, constructions, and explorations involving knowledge. N. Katherine Hayles writes in *How We Became Posthuman*,

> Information, like humanity, cannot exist apart from the embodiment that brings it into being as a material entity in the world; and embodiment is always instantiated, local, and specific. Embodiment can be destroyed, but it cannot be replicated. Once the specific form constituting it is gone, no amount of massaging data will bring it back. This observation is as true of the planet as it is of an individual life-form. As we rush to explore the new vistas that cyberspace has made available for colonization, let us remember the fragility of a material world that cannot be replaced.[5]

In an evanescent world of ideas embedded in a fragile material world, we become artists of fragility and improvisation.

We understand through the lens of our self. In a museum or library, we stand slightly apart and observe our responses and our thinking. After walking deliberately through an exhibition or examining a shelf of written works, we might conduct a tacit inventory of what has just happened.

- How do we begin to respond, when knowledge, evidence, or something new and engaging is before us? We observe our own acts of noticing, pausing, paying attention, using our senses when we are in complex places. We observe the similar acts of others as well as we can.
- We notice what engages us the longest or the most deeply and that we observe or study something within it. How do we examine it? We remind ourselves that mind is a verb, as John Dewey says,[6] and it is moving and lingering over details that seem to seize our eyes.
- What connections come to our minds? We consider memories and old places the experience brings to mind. We make connections to nearby stimuli, to the renewed contexts now flowing anew through our lives, and to the questions we have asked before and are likely to ask again.
- Fragments of language come to us. Concepts and words escape us. What do we read, what do we speak, what do we write down? What mental notes do we attempt to keep? We want to capture or communicate something. What is it?
- What patterns can we see in this experience? Is it like other experiences at other times? Do we find parallel moments among other situations? Do we ask "How" or "Why" or "What if"?

When we become inquirers, we begin to live on our own horizons, not the horizons of a teacher, a leader, or another person, but our own. We behave usefully in the situation because we need to make something of it. Being human beings, we wish to understand it. We construct useful behaviors in response to the gaps and lapses of clarity we encounter. We roam through our past for some parallel observation or the echo of something similar we once experienced.

Between the recollected sensations of what we have seen and felt most vividly in the past and what we are seeing now for the first time, we build bridges. We strive to create a situation that is not fragmented, but whole. When we are learning and thinking *in* the situation, and *about* the situation, our lives are moving forward—we "reach out to create an opening," in Maxine Greene's words—toward something fresh and possible for us.[7] We hope for news, we wait for an illumination, and if no illumination comes, we ask new questions. Unknown by unknown, we renew ourselves. When we are engaged by the situation, we dwell inside it, as Michael Polanyi says; we live in our questions, and we live through our questions.

> Contemplation dissolves the screen, stops our movement through experience and puts us straight into experience; we cease to handle things and become immersed in them. . . . And as we lose ourselves in contemplation, we take on an impersonal life in the objects of our contemplation; while these objects themselves are suffused by a visionary gleam which lends them a new vivid and yet dreamlike reality. It is dreamlike, for it is timeless and without definite spatial location.[8]

In a place that is not a place, we discover ourselves and our powers not simply in the experiences of asking, and in the answers we find, but also in our feeling the need to be here at this moment, living and responding in the presence of the unknown.

Over time, what we come to understand is less a mystery or a revelation than it is an alternative to what we have already known: in every museum, in every library, we see alternative cultures based on different assumptions than our own, or we see the traces of individuals whose thinking is different and creative, and still a part of their time and our own. The more vivid and impressive our experiences of the new, the greater our opportunity to understand alternatives to the bounded situation of the everyday. Immersed in one life, we are invited to think beyond it. It seems to me we are then more likely to act anew, and then to consider anew all the conventional dimensions of our lives.

We are capable of changing in this way over the span of life. We can engage with new experiences as our living world changes. We can come to trust ourselves as learners among other learners. We can come to look at the array of possible places to learn as an assembly of educative resources; we can see other learners as a gathering of models and teachers. Identifying these patterns of association and engagement, we build a life that moves and reflects. We are learners. We build. We observe. We reflect. We move forward.

A memorable, engaging experience that teaches us is an artifact of circumstances: the confluence of a mind with an object, or a setting and a memory, and perhaps another person. Or it is something less concrete. We enter a place that is not a place, but a field of possibility. We are given an opportunity to explore and hypothesize, to imagine and to illuminate, and to trust ourselves as learners. Our one human life is an artifact constructed by how we explore, hypothesize, imagine, illuminate, and trust ourselves. Neither our knowledge nor our hope will follow from either accident or design alone; we grow through the mix. Our great task is to balance and build ourselves, relying on situations we trust, where we can discover independently and sometimes ardently, communicating all the while about the possibilities before us.

We must be variable and vulnerable, or we cannot progress toward integrity. Every time we organize or connect information we illuminate it with our own experiences and dimensions, sometimes with parts of our own pain and at other times with our satisfactions. We bring a memory of another encounter, a connection to the interest and mind of another person, or we bring sudden understanding of depth and possibility. Every time we do this, opening ourselves, we make our understanding different and new: more complex, subtler, better, less conventional, more surprising, more original.

Our long-term changes—maturing, adapting, rethinking, recovering—are ways of arriving at new designs for what we have lived, and what we will live. Perhaps this is learning. This is deeper than textual or analytic thinking or the testing that passes for progress and certainty in the known world. Learning is more intuitive, more self-defining than knowledge we are given. As we are learning, our adjustments and responses are tacit, invisible actions; our systems require us to change, even though we may be silent and clueless as we do. We are always recalibrating our stance, the pitch of our shoulders, our focus on the distance, the tilt of our head, the weave of our path through the traffic of a moving crowd. No rule or practice for *the learner learning* will mean more than this one: keep moving forward, keep the mind in motion. We will not lose these experiences; they are ours because they have come from inside ourselves, from under our own skins.

When we are variable and vulnerable, physical places of change are important to us for the stability and privacy, even the intensity, they provide. From such places we can find a way to change. Insofar as they encourage trust, generative places can strengthen our ways of renewal. This is their promise. In our world, it is knowledge and experience and communication that will best palliate and heal fear and emptiness. When we are fearful we most need a safe place to pause and to think our way forward, to see what lies before us as a gift, and to know how we might come to use it. At least this is my view of human beings engaged in the works of lives.

My work in thinking and teaching about libraries and museums has caused me to become an advocate for the constructive situations where reflective learning can occur. I hope to remind and encourage every person to think of the private work of intellectual life as conversing, reading, and observing whenever it is possible to break away even briefly from our constraints. Museums and libraries exist in part to show us this possible part of our selves. They help us to remind each other that, in all the work of human growth and exchange, we can be artisans and craftspeople grounded in our common aspirations, and in kindness and generosity. I believe that when we are strong enough to fulfill our promise as individual learners, we also expand our capability for affection, for teaching, and for parenting. We use our greatest tools of mind and heart to alter our perspectives, our thinking, and our social lives. These alterations assure us that we are, from time to time to time, different persons because of what we have experienced.

I have served as a library school educator, and as a school teacher and academic librarian, but no new electronic information tool nor any of its possibilities will cause me to disavow the truths I have crafted over time, even in an age that wants to contradict them. I am not a Luddite; no library user or museum advocate can be. But I have never ceded my fascination with paper, with tools of knowing, with handheld experiences, and the knowledge that will remain in them when I have left. I try to cultivate a learner's stable process in a wired, facile, bright, and sometimes driven setting. It is essential, now, for me to see the art in my slowness and deliberation, the strength in paper, and the value in complexity that is not produced by technology. As many who are close to me know, I find myself to be puzzled, remote, skeptical, dull about most things, at a loss, fearful. And yet I know that the mind is not about speed; it is about art.

Tools allow new ways to consider the possible, to find and evaluate content, and then (if they are good, generative tools) they lead us on, toward further discovery and reflection. The great unknowns do not change much. The questions that last longest are best. For all learners, the mind and not the machine must be the guide, the urge toward theory and system, the source of synthesis and order. The mind is our own embodied artist of complexity, power, and skill. Nothing tangible does this guiding for us. Authorship of this kind always resides in hiding, within us. We bring knowledge into the world; we embody it, perishable as we are, perishable as it is.

The situation we require holds an unconditional invitation to explore freely and receive assistance, to ask original questions and experience unscripted, evolving responses that lead us to more questions than we originally had. Learning requires convivial settings where stories can be exchanged and experiences can be confirmed—where flexible alternatives can be suggested, and strategies can be compared. In this situation for learning, conversations about our experiences alter those experiences, clarify, deepen, and revise them, and allow us to use them in new circumstances.

Each of us needs to learn in this situation, or in one that matches it in essential ways, at least once in our lives, but we know that such convivial experiences are rare. Perhaps our work begins when we break through the proliferating insularities of contemporary culture in order to demonstrate the benefits of conversation in a community of others. Every learning is proven in such a community.

When we have broken through, our work is to remind each other that we might yet become different and more reflective persons, and through our most generative institutions we might yet find the best of ourselves.

The world I describe in this collection is purposeful but difficult to envision or achieve. For every living person, I hypothesize that there is a lifelong constructive process of learning, changing, or becoming, and for each person I hypothesize a series of lived experiences responsive to that process. We cannot live without responding to this need or we lose the capacity to become. Learning occurs when our unfinished issues and our useful experiences fit together and alter each other. Our lives are defined by these alterations and their tensions: we open to something new, some promised expansion or self-rescue, and we find that it has brought us something we could not have expected, for reflection and possible embrace. We act to learn in barely visible ways, and in reflection we find that our acts have left invisible traces.

The essays in *A Place Not a Place* include extensions and reinvestments of several themes central to *The Promise of Cultural Institutions*. The first essay here, published as it originally appeared in *Teachers College Record*, is in fact the earliest of my publications articulating the importance of questions, the configuration of learning in cultural institutions, and the extraordinary challenge of being alone as we learn within them. It is republished here because it both summarizes my beginning decade of studies and field experiences and is the foundation of my subsequent thinking over fifteen years.

During the 1990s my work was primarily teaching, managing a graduate program, and contributing to the successes of people other than myself. Perhaps the essays "What I Saw in the Museum," "What I Read in the Library," and "Wanting, At Ten" are ways for me to recover and describe the founding impulses of my thinking after those years of silence, exploration, and hope. (I now plan to turn my attention to the journals I kept during my earliest museum field visits, starting in 1983, to recover my first reflections as an adult learner and educator, as I found unexpected treasures and thoughts in abundance.)

I am frequently asked to think and speak, in specific situations, to professional library and museum audiences, staff members, and volunteers. As a scholar I write in professional journals as well. The essays "Rescuing the User," "Reading Beyond the Museum," "Five Thoughtful Exercises," "Observing Collaboration," and "What Do We Want," are my ways to encourage changes in practice through new behaviors. They address practice based on the challenges of learning and guiding others as learners. I think they might inspire applications across all cultural institutions. I know that every one of the ideas in these five essays has come from my work and observations among many institutions, but also from my incomparable experiences as a teacher of aspiring professionals. It surprises me to notice that I am nearly in my fifth decade of teaching, striving to transmit to others a responsibility to lead cognitive growth in every encounter, through our practices and advocacy. Though I now see my path as a series of accidents and errors, I am grateful to have been a teacher, and especially to have been a teacher of librarians.

The essays that close this book have origins in my own advocacy. I know that the challenge of professional service in librarianship and museum work is unified: my colleagues in museums and libraries will strive every day to resolve through practice the tension between our great institutions and their unrealized possibilities in the lives of its users. This tension will never be resolved, but it will always be inviting; it is the great unfinished issue of every institution in our democracy. We will always speak of promise and the possible in the place that is not a place.

When I am privileged to speak among professional audiences whose vocations have matched my own, I hope to answer their unspoken questions: "What matters? What are the tensions and challenges? Where is the beginning of change?" But I often feel at a loss after I have spoken, believing that it is never enough merely to give questions to others, as I tend to do. It is far more vital and useful to be a living instrument of transformation in an institution, using questions as levers or tools. My envy of those who practice in libraries and museums will always challenge me. I am grateful to have spoken among such people; much of this book holds what I have said or have wanted to say on those occasions as their colleague. I thank them for their generosity, inspiration, and presence.

Thinking of Shakespeare's thirty-seventh sonnet, I offer this book with love and devotion to my daughters Eve and Anna. *I take all my comfort of thy worth and truth.* It is also given to my students, several thousand now, over four decades. *I in thy abundance am sufficed / And by a part of all thy glory live.* Every good and lasting thing I do follows from the generous gift of trust I have been given by others. Thank you for thinking with me.

Look what is best, that best I wish in thee.

Carrboro, North Carolina
April 2006

NOTES

1. Howard Gardner, *Frames of Mind: The Theory of Multiple Intelligences* (New York: Basic Books, 1983), 39.

2. Gardner, *Frames of Mind*, 35.

3. Howard Gruber, "Courage and Cognitive Growth in Children and Scientists," in Milton Schwebel and Jane Raph, eds., *Piaget in the Classroom* (New York: Basic Books, 1973), 79.

4. Gruber, "Courage and Cognitive Growth," 80.

5. N. Katherine Hayles, *How We Became Posthuman: Virtual Bodies in Cybernetics, Literature and Informatics* (Chicago: University of Chicago Press, 1999), 49.

6. John Dewey. *Art as Experience* [*The Later Works, 1925–1953*. Vol. 10: 1934], ed. by Jo Ann Boydston (Carbondale: Southern Illinois University Press, 1987), 268.

7. Maxine Greene, *The Dialectic of Freedom* (New York: Teachers College Press, 1988), 11.

8. Michael Polanyi, *Personal Knowledge* (Chicago: University of Chicago Press, 1958), 197.

1

THE COGNITIVE MANAGEMENT OF CULTURAL INSTITUTIONS*

When thoughtful people experience vivid information, poignant issues, or their own unfamiliar reflections in museums and libraries, they reach to grasp more, see farther, and understand critically, beyond themselves.

- At the Jewish Museum in New York City, an adult granddaughter wheels her grandmother's chair through an exhibition titled "Getting Comfortable in New York: The American Jewish Home, 1880–1950," asking questions. Did you own a piano like this one? Was your apartment this small? Did you observe holidays there? The grandmother's responses are clear and specific: not this kind; yes, and with wallpaper like this, too; no, usually at my aunt's, sometimes at home. The younger woman asks more questions, each designed to specify, distinguish, and understand the grandmother's experience as a Jewish woman, her foremother in the city.
- At the American Museum of the Moving Image in Astoria, New York, a museum user observes and plays forty-seven different video arcade games, assembled in chronological order from Computer Space (1971) and Pong (1972), through Space Invaders (1978) and Asteroids (1979) to Out Run (1986) and Narc (1988). The user moves through the gallery, participating in a history of popular technology, redefining his previous notions of play in twentieth-century America, and challenging concepts static since childhood.

---

*This essay was published in the Fall 1991 issue of *Teachers College Record*, and is included unchanged here as evidence of my founding thoughts in contemplation of museums, libraries, and their users. Most of the themes that inspire me now began in this essay.

1

- At the Webber Resource Center in Chicago's Field Museum of Natural History, the museum user emerges from extensive collections of Native American objects, stands before an information desk, and asks a question about Southwest Native American song. After consulting with a museum assistant on duty, the inquirer selects a videotape of original singing and dancing; it is shown privately in one of four small video rooms. After, the user examines the musical instruments heard in this performance, reads books and newspapers about contemporary tribal music, and attends a concert by Chilean folk musicians playing informally in an adjacent gallery.

- At the Indianapolis Children's Museum—called a museum *with*, not simply for, children—a museum user enters a gallery titled "Teens Speak Out On Issues," and sees exhibits devoted to teenage pregnancy, child abuse, alcohol and drug addiction, AIDS, world peace, and school. He photographs these and copies portions of the wall texts into a small notebook. The words on the walls, as well as the issues, displays, construction, and presentation, were accomplished by students invited by the museum to identify the matters at the heart of their experience, and then trained by museum specialists to design and build these displays. Childhood and youth are further redefined here, made less distant, more distinct and troubling to the user.

- At the American Museum of Natural History in New York City, in the Hall of South American Peoples, a museum user finds objects relating to child initiation rites among tribal peoples of the Amazon. These include objects used in clitoridectomies and the application of fire ants to children's bodies. Nearby the user finds displays describing patterns of drug and alcohol use among tribal peoples and is led to reflect on norms and instances of parallel behavior in American society.

- At the Rochester, New York, Museum and Science Center, the user pauses near the threshold of an exhibition titled "At the Western Door: Seneca Indians, Europeans and Americans in the Genesee Valley," where the "Native American View" and the "European View" of deities and humans, the land, and trade and commerce are closely juxtaposed. This comparison continues throughout the exhibit, presenting evidence and telling the story of the transformation of the region spiritually, physically, and economically through close and explicit comparisons of the character and nature of each group.

- At a space called The Sixth Floor, in the Texas School Book Depository Building in Dallas, a museum user hears gunfire he first understood more than a quarter century before, and reconstructs his knowledge of the life, death, and memory of an assassinated president. The user hears and reads about the contexts—legal, social, local, global, political, personal—that permanently surround November 22–25, 1963. The user records his impressions and memories in a large public loose-leaf book. His writing follows the rantings of a conspiracy theorist, an expression of sorrow from a citizen of Dallas, and a child's handwritten questions. Later, the observer writes privately about the feeling of abiding generational loss and disappointment suddenly discovered in himself. He describes his equally sudden astonishment at having been there, having seen what the assassin saw through the window over Dealey Plaza, having recovered memories that, until that moment, had been lost.

In cultural institutions—museums and libraries—moments of redefining and reorganizing our ideas, and for breaking-through and transforming our images of ourselves, are immanent in all things. Though they are situations for learning in the public frame, cultural institutions induce private moments for reflecting, revising, and reinterpreting the invisible and often ambiguous texts that over time compose one life. Information in the museum (or library, zoo, or garden), the clear and immediate presence of sensory data, the vivid pertinence of complex objects, and the exhilaration of empirical inquiry and conceptual innovation—all of these challenge the constraints and routines of everyday life. Their nearness is extraordinary; it expands the channels of conventional perception. As the learner perceives the surfaces and contents of things, organizes patterns, contemplates origins, explores concepts of time and environment, and differentiates among ideas and images, the surrounding cultural institution becomes a critical agency in the construction of an individual intellectual life. In these situations for learning, the information given and the objects seen can have a formative influence on a private cognitive system. When these institutions touch the lives of thoughtful persons, the future is changed.

This essay uses the term "cultural institution" to evoke a number of settings that share common strands of mission and effect. My observations over the past decade suggest that it is useful to see museums, libraries, zoological and botanical gardens, historic preservations and reconstructions, even public parks and natural resources, in a large and inclusive frame. It seems clear that they are similarly founded and driven, and that they inspire similar cognitive acts. Perhaps they are the treasuries of a culture, but they are not passive; their educative tasks involve design, transmission, and cognition. Any advocacy for critical thinkers in cultural institutions will matter broadly across settings, no matter how they are defined nor what treasure they hold.

Among the purposes of this essay are to make clear the shared cognitive dimensions of these settings, to suggest that they create greatly similar rather than essentially different situations for transmitting information, and by implication to clarify how different in these dimensions cultural institutions are from schools. Another purpose is to encourage a critical understanding of public cultural institutions as well, and so to expand not only the terms and thoughts applied to museums and libraries, but also to enlarge the potential for public discourse about their analysis and criticism.

These observations are drawn from nearly two decades as a professional librarian, educator, observer, scholar, and consultant in libraries and museums, led by several guiding questions. What might be learned here—and what is expected of the learner? What thinking is supported by the experiences encountered here? What are the dimensions and applications of these thoughts? What differences might this experience cause in an individual life? Responding to these questions—observing and documenting situations for learning; comparing, analyzing, and reflecting on learning experiences—has led to this perspective. Over hundreds of occasions, the observer's attention has been systematically drawn to experiences of language in cultural institutions, to the assumptions embedded in their invitations to learners, and to elements of design and juxtaposition that illuminate institutional logics. Where these logics, messages, and designs suggest particular sensitivity to the situation of the learner, the observer has been rapt, and his questions have been constant: What is the nature of the invitation given to learners here, and what is the quality of the giving?

A TENSION OF CONSCIOUSNESS

To begin, the reader might imagine standing at the entrance to the American Museum of Natural History, the New York Public Library, the Metropolitan Museum of Art, or any other cultural institution summoned to mind, about to enter for the first time. Briefly suspended there, the reader might usefully dwell in the acute but exquisite tension that tends to surround the intellect among arrays of enticing choices, all suggesting the vision, expression, and knowledge of human beings, all carrying the promise of something new. Captured there for more than the moment—in the nearness of inviting masterworks, at the edge of some reconstructed era or evocative image—the reader may feel that a transforming experience is at hand, if it can be found, seized, and fully lived. Berger and Luckmann refer to a "tension of consciousness" that characterizes moments of this kind: an awareness of an unusual world unfolding for us alone, comprising multiple realities, each demanding its own transition, each implying its own context and complexity, and each available to us briefly.[1] The problem for the museum or library user, pausing at the door, is to understand this moment as an evanescent tension of consciousness, and to become a participant in its exploration and use. How does a learner resolve this vivid tension and step thoughtfully forward?

A colleague once suggested that this uneasiness should be called "bewilderness," a combination of stimuli, intentions, and questions that act together under the constraints of using a museum or library. In the Metropolitan Museum, for example, bewilderness could include an awareness of the extension and scope of this encyclopedic place, its infinite combination of paths, the subtle continuities of these paths across cultures and themes, the allusive scholarly or curatorial subtexts embedded in the density of labels, and the particular richness of the offered examples among all possible examples. Again, to cite Berger and Luckmann, this is a realm we know to be filled with "finite provinces of meaning," constellations and arrays that, gallery by gallery, evince a structure of critical choices and a network of themes.[2] However vague our resources or weak our vision, we may sense a horizon beyond the trees: an organizing genius, a sensibility, a theory or design, a guiding constitution or shaping intellect that tells us nothing is here by accident.

But we are typically on our own in the museum or library, using our own compasses as thinkers and explainers, deeply dependent on our own genius for inquiry and reflection. Standing at this edge, we carry tacit structures and guiding stars: memories of past museums; fragments recollected from college courses; a conversation with someone long dead; memories of faces and landscapes; images out of childhood; the convulsive imprint of personal turmoil; and other inspirations hidden beneath the multilayered tissues of memory. Enfolded among these ghostly strands of information and feeling are ideas, needs, or questions of the moment, the thoughts that bring us to this edge today. Each of our faint fragments holds promise or emptiness; but each causes us to see that we are not here by accident either. Framed in this way—a living complexity of images and experiences verging on a designed complexity of objects and texts—the learner stands and pauses, and then moves the mind into the unfolding array.

CULTURAL INSTITUTIONS AND
THE CRITICALLY MINDFUL LIFE

This essay considers the epistemic acts and relationships between cultural institutions and the critically mindful lives of their users, lives that stand in the flow of information—and are sometimes carried forward, over rocks into eddies and pools. It is assumed here that critical thinkers are stimulated by this flow, its tensions, its risks of mind. Mihaly Csikszentmihalyi describes a flow experience as "one of complete involvement of the actor with his activity," an unusual state of engagement beyond the everyday.[3] For several reasons, the idea of flow can be usefully applied to the critical thinker in the cultural institution.

The situation for learning in cultural institutions—inviting, astonishing choices, provocative and extraordinary juxtapositions—educes a reflective process, polishes a cognitive mirror for the examination of images, thoughts, and beliefs. This examination is a critical process; as the user observes, considers, and attends to objects and ideas, the scrutiny of governing assumptions is required. Why is this here? How does this connect? What does it mean to my interests and my life? Such thinking tends to consider alternatives to the conventional. The critical thinker enters the immediate presence of the evidence and contemplates an open door of possible meanings among texts or artifacts that by definition stand apart from the commonplace. This thinking recognizes changes in the features and patterns on the face of experience; it uses the familiar to examine the unknown. As information expands, perspectives change; reflections may reframe the memories and assumptions of an entire life. Or it may resolve unclarity, attuning dissonances, and easing constraints in an evolving life.

The most effective cultural institutions capture the complex extremities of human experience and knowledge; with varying degrees of success, they combine, order, and illuminate them for public access. Perhaps we create and sustain knowledge structures and information systems of this kind because, as John Gardner says, "We are problem-solvers by nature—problem-seekers, problem-requirers."[4] Our culture may use such institutions to contain permanently the artifacts, texts, and records it wishes to hold as forms of experience and knowledge; it also uses them to keep at hand the information we require if we are ever to feel at home in time and space. For their users, such settings offer new information to lives of continuous growth. In them, human beings can consider, compare, integrate, and think beyond the evidences of experience. Inherently, cultural institutions are public places intended for learners, and for lives of self-invention and pursuit. At their best, they are forums for communication, independent learning, and self-presentation, intended for the living of life on one's own horizon, and yet informed by the horizons of others.

Museums and libraries are institutions for the mindful life. Ellen J. Langer has described mindfulness as a state of engagement with the environment and its constant flow of information, a flow that expands the capacity of the receiver while diminishing the effects of entropy. Langer sees mindfulness as

> [a] state of alertness and lively awareness . . . specifically manifested in typical ways. Generally, mindfulness is expressed in active information processing, characterized by cognitive differentiation: the creation of categories and distinctions. The act of creating distinctions tacitly creates new categories and vice versa. . . . Mindfulness may be seen as creating (noticing) multiple perspectives, or being aware of context. When in this state, the person is becoming more and more differentiated while differentiating the external world.[5]

We might say that museums and libraries—institutions rife with schemata, constructs, taxonomies, and perspectives—serve mindfulness by holding the changing world constant and offering a form or structure for it, so the mind can grasp, reflect, and move forward within a design. (Think of the great and memorable Blue Whale, suspended from the ceiling in the Hall of Ocean Life at the American Museum of Natural History, as a fragment of that complexity held still for us to see, and consider how easily the mind moves on, far beyond Central Park West, to an informed image of the creature in its depths.)

Mindlessness, Langer says, sustains entropy; it is a "state of reduced attention . . . expressed in behavior that is rigid and rule-governed rather than rule-guided. The individual becomes mindlessly trapped by categories that were previously created when in a mindful mode. This entrapment limits people both physiologically and behaviorally."[6] Fully realized, the lifelong processes of information discovery and intellectual growth oppose mindlessness through the construction of an independent learning life. It might be said that cultural institutions exist for the self-construction of a life without mindless entrapment. The critical passages that forge a generative intellect appear more likely to be realized among the cultural continuities and encyclopedic information of cultural institutions than in any school. Museums and libraries stand as *the* public instruments for self-renewal in a society where much teaching and schooling misses entirely the life span message, telling little or nothing about how to respond to personal emptiness and uncompleted thoughts as they are encountered in adult experience.

To be an adult is to be reminded every day of the unfinished learning and unresolved intellectual issues, some begun years ago, that stay and increase with age. New conceptions of the world are documented and framed daily in the pages of *The New York Times*; and with these new frames may come an awareness of our personal illiteracy and ignorance among the complex texts that influence one life. Living on the edges of these events, but deeply aware of them, we are challenged to articulate new definitions of the world, to clarify the distinctions we can understand, and to respond to the challenges and uncertainties we feel. Critical thinking begins here, in the search for resonances, semblances of order, and recognitions as we stand on the verge of change. Is it reasonable to suggest that most adults stand in proximity to an undertow of mindlessness, a loss of power in the waves of life, a restive compliance with the tides of routine? Is it not also reasonable to suggest that, through afternoons and evenings in the proximities of libraries and museums, one life can be challenged and awakened by the possibilities of inquiry, continuity, and critical innovation?

In a world that demands complex cognition it is easily possible to waive independent reflection, yielding to kinds of thought Jack Mezirow refers to as "epistemic distortions": thinking that there is a single answer to a complex issue, rather than any number of provisional, discourse-based ideas; perceiving the social world to be fixed and immutable; interpreting the world concretely when abstract thought is required; finding meaning in empiricism alone.[7] Mezirow describes critical reflection in problem solving as a form of thought that attends to the coherence of our assumptions, the completeness of our knowledge, and the quality of the empirical processes we use to verify and understand our experiences.[8] These moments are critical because they involve decisions, reassessments, and actions for learning that combine intellectual strategies, processes, and personal values. When we reflect in the pursuit of meanings (Mezirow calls this "communicative learning"), we require coherence among our concepts and values, accuracy in the decoding of messages, and a logic in ordering concepts that allows valid insights to be drawn.

> Communicative learning is less a matter of testing hypotheses than of searching, often intuitively, for themes and metaphors by which to fit the unfamiliar into a meaning perspective, so that an interpretation in context becomes possible.[9]

As we look at the unknown solutions embedded in problems and the unknown meanings embedded in unfamiliar messages, we are cognitively self-aware; thinking toward coherence, we regulate the information we receive and attend to our own cognition as we use it.[10]

Thinking for oneself within a community of discourse and inquiry is the hallmark of adult independent learning; critical thinking is a positive, productive, and constructive process, leading the thinker toward authentic self-awareness and the articulation of living personal values. Definitions of critical thinking make clear its essential place in any discourse about adult learning and thought, and they suggest its special consequence in the contexts of museums, libraries, and other cultural institutions.[11]

- Critical thinking involves the integration of complex events and information related to living issues; it is an incremental process, not easily contained or resolved.
- Critical thinking is self-induced and self-controlled. Its forms are variable and adaptive, depending on the contexts, issues, and kinds of discourse in specific situations.
- Critical thinking is pervasive in the life of the thinker. It is about both cognition and emotion; it challenges assumptions, increases awareness of causes, contexts and constraints, and emphasizes the imagination, exploration, and contemplation of alternatives to existing conditions.
- Critical thinking engages the narrow, private world of the thinker—often involving profound questions, indirection, and doubt—with a public world of dialectic and dialogue. The presence of questions and errors are seen as certain indicators of learning.

Definitions emphasize that the critical thinker is a strategist and a diagnostician, tending toward the construction of whole configurations of the world—but cautious and reflective. Richard Paul speaks of "tentative graspings of a whole guiding us in understanding its parts."[12]

While critical thinking is often thought to be triggered by personal distress or challenge, it is more likely the peak experience, the moment of insight, the flow of integration or coherence that inspires reappraisal and raises new questions. At moments of achievement and change, we tend to feel powerful. When we encounter promising alternative ideas, we are ready to explore them. When we are influenced by gifted exemplars or promising situations for learning, we may be inspired. Moreover, at those times we may have specific, real, and possible models of transformation before us. Our criteria for relevance are extended. We may deem new classes of objects and information to be interesting and useful in our lives; we may develop new standards for being present and engaged. We may see excellence where we once saw nothing. Stephen Brookfield writes, "When we think critically we become aware of the diversity of values, behaviors, social structures, and artistic forms in the world."[13] Critical thinking leads us toward the edges of our frames and then assists us to dissolve those frames as other structures take form.

It is possible to understand critical thinking in the museum or library as the cognitive management of cultural institutions, a reflective process comprising a series of interpretive moments. Museums and libraries create problems for which the only solution is critical thinking. As certainly as they are real and tactile environments, cultural institutions are also reflective spaces, intentionally symbolic, encoded, and intellectual. To find one's way, one must think, and typically one must do this alone. Museums and libraries present every user with the problem of acting with purpose in order to construct meaning.

CULTURAL INSTITUTIONS AS INSTRUMENTS OF MINDFULNESS

The situation for critical thinking in cultural institutions involves the presence of an accessible array of objects and information, typically systematized in some form of thematic or physical order. The ordering of this array may involve simple naming or the provision of detailed contexts and supporting concepts. Further, beyond simple identifications, accurate information is present in the forms of written or spoken words, illustrations, maps, or schemata. The museum or library and the mediating surround are purposive: the designed array follows from a series of selections and juxtapositions, based on pertinent connoisseurship or expertise, and carried out systematically over time. The integrity of any collection and its surrounding interpretation comes to our attention through such variable characteristics as wholeness, balance, and quality.

Among collected objects and information, the apotheosis of the cultural institution as an instrument for critical thinking appears wherever the institution communicates respect for the reflective mind. It appears, for example, in the texts of signs and explanations, labels, and brochures; in the logic, articulation, and coherence of themes; in the ease of transition from the array to its implications beyond the institution. The conditions for critical thinking in any cultural institution are not hidden. Immediately, the human being in the array confronts the need to make choices. With what ease is the user encouraged to strike out into innovative experiential and cognitive realms? How readily are alternatives to the familiar presented to the learner? The situation for thinking critically in any cultural institution is defined by the inherent presence of intellectual challenge in the array.

The learner in the cultural institution is engaged in a mindful system of logics, however private they may be. Depending on the newness or the risk of the venture, the nature of an exploratory process in the museum or library will depend on several kinds of knowledge involving language, history, and a sensitivity to relationships. This process will involve a (perhaps tacit) system for observing and documenting information. The user's journey may be direct, or it may be circuitous; it may create opportunities to seek explanations and advice; it may demand supplementary journeys toward a full understanding of contexts.

Cultural institutions are exemplary instruments of mindfulness and critical thinking because they typically encompass a range of alternative visions, experiences, and information. They are broadly and freely accessible across cultures; they invite the attention, self-expression, and free communication of users without the constraints associated with schools. And, unlike schools, cultural institutions are incomplete without a participative human imagination. While all cultural institutions are not equal in size or mission, nor equally accessible to users, they exist as strongly egalitarian agencies devoted to the provision of data and experiences apart from everyday resources. They hold the record of human achievements and acts and their information systems inform mindful constructions of the world. Cultural institutions create situations that induce language and discourse; these tend to induce self-renewal and change.

Cultural institutions are also common places used daily and freely by diverse public learners seeking accurate information, expansive intellectual experiences, or usable guidance for the conduct of life. Museums and libraries are formative because they make possible private transformations through discovery, exploration, and reflection beyond the information at hand. Adaptive, expansive, and comprehensive, organized for systematic use, cultural institutions stand against fragmentation. They provide opportunities to see entire collections of objects or ideas, and in them it is possible to discover themes and patterns that can form whole new pieces of understanding. Concepts, eras, revolutions, movements are transformed in them to objects and information that capture and communicate. At their best, cultural institutions are settings for dialogues and transactions among companions, verifications of evidence, the drawing of inferences and diagnoses, speculations about authenticity, uninterrupted reflections, expressions of inquiry, and, in a phrase borrowed from Maxine Greene, "intergenerational continuity."[14]

Professor Greene's important attention to "public spaces," settings where people can come together to share their stories and lived realities, is especially important because it emphasizes the potential uses of cultural institutions as resources where lives can be lived with increasing self-definition.[15] As public spaces, museums and libraries are environments where human beings can come to understand the fresh and unroutinized parts of themselves: their curiosities, their continuing, unfinished issues, and unarticulated needs to learn. The cultural institution responds to its users by providing structures and opportunities for the exploration and communication of literacies, personal histories, and cultural differences. Such forums invite challenging alternative stances toward experience; they provide access to the diverse cultural texts, artifacts, and contexts that confer meaning in one life over time. Speaking about the educative value of urban public spaces, Richard Sennett recently said, "The classic ideal of a public space was that it was a place of truth. It was where people understood other people in society by talking to them. . . . Successful spaces prompt people to believe that something's possible there, that the space is not complete and that they are invited to complete it."[16] He might well have been speaking about the museum or the library, where critical thinking and dialogue have a double effect: they complete the surrounding structure as they connect participants to objects, information, and each other.

THE INVITATION TO KNOW

Cognitive mastery in the cultural institution is not based only on an expanding catalog in the mind, but on sensitized knowing, critically developed when an intelligence works within a knowledge structure, using its information to expand and deepen perceptions. Intimacy with a collection helps to construct the foundation for what Jerome Bruner calls going beyond the information given.[17] That is, apart from the discovery of specific content or experiences, the mindful probing of the library or museum and its knowledge structures allows a learner to forge a personal intellectual style and to develop patterns of approach to the problems of cultural learning. Given the insularity and blandness of much contemporary life, the most important dimensions of thought fostered in cultural institutions may have to do with the learner's integrity and strength of mind in the presence of first-hand experiences. As systems of objects and information, cultural institutions necessarily invite constructive mental acts.

In "Art as a Mode of Knowing," Bruner alludes to "the self-rewarding experience of connection,"[18] often accomplished through the use of metaphors as bridges between private and public thinking. Bruner says that, apart from the direct, object-centered approach to art works, there is a second, more intuitive approach to the experience of art: "At the fringes of awareness, a flow of rich and surprising fantasy, a tangled reticle of associations that gives fleeting glimpses of past occasions, of disappointments and triumphs, of pleasures and unpleasures."[19] This "fringe" is where the intellect leaps, where mindful risks are taken, and where personal vision is illuminated through direct experiences. Engaging in thought that is "more symphonic than logical, one theme suggesting the next," the user brings to experience "a matrix of life that is uniquely his own."[20] To use Csikszentmihalyi's term, these are "autotelic" optimal experiences.

> The autotelic experience, or flow, lifts the course of life to a different level. Alienation gives way to involvement, enjoyment replaces boredom, helplessness turns into a feeling of control, and psychic energy works to reinforce the sense of self, instead of being lost in the service of external goals. When experience is intrinsically rewarding life is justified in the present, instead of being held hostage to a hypothetical future gain.[21]

Pursuits that flow from engaged caring can give an adult life intellectual design, a pattern of meanings that stay fresh. Similarly, critical thoughts and acts, flowing from a hunger to know, become landmarks in a mindful life. Chasing good thoughts—edgy, riddling, enigmatic thoughts—extends and exercises the ability to think.

Independent learners about to enter the Metropolitan Museum or New York Public Library should expect a rapid change of stimuli, various degrees of confusion, anonymity among unknown companions, ambiguity of meanings, and uncertain closure. Amid ambiguities, the learner must make choices, design a path, or ask a question in order to move ahead into the stimuli present. Against the potential for cognitive chaos in these acts— where impression overwhelms impression and serendipity can overturn any plan—the value of an ordered approach is clear.

The cognitive management of experience in cultural institutions involves an evolution of attention that includes the following elements:

- The presence of a thoughtful, persistent question or tendency toward curiosity as the learner enters the cultural institution.
- Expansion of this single, moving question into a constellation of questions—all of them in motion.
- Out of these questions, the construction of an inquiry that leads the learner on, organizing experiences in patterns.

- The use of a system of documentation or commentary: companion-ate discussions; use of a notebook, camera, and/or tape recorder.
- Regular pauses to reflect and redesign the planned use of the cultural setting.
- An inventory of ideas to pursue in the future, using other resources, among other learners, in this or other institutions.

These experiences educe logic and process; they follow the learner beyond the institution; they occur in public situations; they are examples of making sense of a lived world. To be a learner in this setting is to reflect on the known and the unknown, and to manage the interaction between the two.

CULTURAL INSTITUTIONS, CRITICAL THINKING, AND THE CONDUCT OF LIFE

How does critical thinking in cultural institutions affect the conduct of life? First, it alters the proximity between the inquiring learner and the pertinent evidence, and so reduces the influence of second-hand discourse. Whatever image or text we find before us, our presence permits us to find and ask the best questions we can, allows immediate, authentic feelings to flow over us, encourages us to observe and record information as our own. Present, we can explore Bruner's "tangled reticle of associations." As Maxine Greene writes in "The Art of Being Present":

> There is no such phenomenon as a second-hand experience with a Cezanne landscape or a Stevens poem or a Woody Allen film. We can never send someone else to see it for us and come back and report. Not only are we required to be there; we are required to be there as active and conscious beings, allowing the energies of perceiving and imagining and feeling to move out to the works at hand, to bring them into life.[22]

Second, critical thinking in cultural institutions, following the intellectual nature and character of these settings, requires distanced, independent re-flection as the basis for informing acts and attention to objects. By nurtur-ing this deliberative style, the museum or the library undoes some of the damages to personal autonomy that follow from the pervasive control of in-dependent learning in most public education. Wherever attention is under individual control it cannot be easily seized by an authority; in museums and libraries, our awareness of complexity cannot be diluted by formal, acon-textual, reductive classroom discourse. Unlike experience in schools, deliberate learning in the cultural institution is an opportunity for change through "situated cognition," characterized by John Seely Brown and his associates as situations where "The activity in which knowledge is developed and deployed . . . is not separable from or ancillary to learning and cognition. Nor is it neutral. Rather, it is an integral part of what is learned. Situations might be said to co-produce knowledge through activity."[23] Cognitive acts in museums and libraries constitute by definition direct participation in knowledge itself—they are acts of cognition in a situation where knowledge and thought matter deeply.

Brown and his associates, borrowing from D. N. Perkins's *Knowledge as Design*, assume that conceptual knowledge can be thought of as tools that "can only be fully understood through use, and using them entails both changing the user's view of the world and adopting the belief system of the culture in which they are used."

> People who use tools actively rather than just acquire them . . . build an increasingly rich implicit understanding of the world in which they use the tools and of the tools themselves. The understanding, both of the world and of the tool, continually changes as a result of their interaction. Learning and acting are interestingly indistinct, learning being a continuous, life-long process resulting from acting in situations.[24]

Such activities, the authors go on to say, are authentic, in contrast to activities transferred and "hermetically sealed within the self-confirming culture of the school," where they are encoded with a formal syntax and diction that surgically separates original experience from supportive contexts.[25] Worse, by empowering teachers as authorities, the sealed culture of the school tends to disempower individual learners from entering situations where their own choices matter. It fails as well to model or reward critical self-discovery.

Third, critical thinking in the presence of objects and texts deeply expands and alters the flow of information through a life. This confers a textural change. Information slows the life down, speeds it up, slams it into the wall, aims it into the past and future while anchoring it more firmly in the here and now. In contrast to the pupil in Gary Larson's cartoon who raises his hand and asks, "Mr. Osborn, may I be excused? My brain is full," Ellen Langer says that mindfulness expands capacities, increases thirsts, makes it more difficult to be bored, and leads the learner toward increasingly complex forms of attention. "When people look for something," Langer writes, "they are surely more likely to find it than if they do not even think to question whether or not it is possible."[26] Simply being present and looking around can create essential changes in information. Serendipitous discoveries are never pure accidents; if one wishes to be informed, it is useful to spend as much time as possible where the information is. When serendipity strikes, it is a reward for being present, and for being mindful.

Fourth, critical cognitive experiences in cultural institutions create landmarks, reference points, watershed experiences that become permanent parts of an individual's repertoire of performing data. They permit the learner to take a vivid experience into the future, and use its meanings there like the tools Brown and his associates allude to. Wolfgang Iser writes about literary texts that they "initiate 'performances' of meaning rather than actually formulating meanings themselves." Further, the same concept of performance might apply to all cultural knowledge: "Without the participation of the individual . . . there can be no performance."[27] Critical thought, when seen as a performance of clarification, verification, or interpretation, underscores not only the immediate relevance of a powerful experience, but it also offers more permanent constructs for use beyond the moment. Bruner cites Iser's remarks in *The Act of Reading* that "readers have both a strategy and a repertoire that they bring to bear on a text,"[28] and this may characterize critical cognitive acts as well. Just as in libraries we encounter powerful texts, in museums we encounter powerful objects or have insightful conversations with companions; these enable us to open parts of ourselves and create (or construct or perform) new meanings for our futures. One way to estimate the relative power of a cultural institution is to consider if it drives us, feeling and thinking, to "perform" thoughts we recognize as new to us.

The final effect of critical thinking in the cultural setting on the conduct of one life is the awareness of continuity and connection it suggests. The individual inquirer in the library or museum stands both in the shadows and at the shoulders of others. Critical thinking is not the isolated act of an individual communicant, but a form of participation in the construction of bridges among communities of persons, their knowledge and experiences. Bruner writes, "A culture itself comprises an ambiguous text that is constantly in need of interpretation by those who participate in it."[29] And Mezirow writes "education for adults may be understood as centrally involved in creating and facilitating dialogic communities to enable learners to engage in rational discourse and action."[30] Meaning comes from negotiation and discourse, toward (in the words of Csikszentmihalyi) "purpose, resolution and harmony."[31]

From the moment of entrance, the contemplative user of a cultural institution is negotiating: choosing a personal stance toward the information array, selecting the means to reconstruct it as a personal map, and designing the paths to be taken through it. It is in the negotiation of this critical passage that the reality of cultural experience is to be found: not in the arrival, not wholly in the objects or texts at hand, but in the flow of thought and language we use to understand what we discover in them. For the learner, the art of performing one's own meanings in cultural institutions lies in selecting, combining, and balancing the contexts we carry stored within us. It involves grasping richness in the texts we find, and the discovery among these messages of our own authentic values. Cultural institutions are environments that stimulate and sustain self-informing human systems.

THE SITUATION OF THE CRITICAL THINKER IN THE CULTURAL INSTITUTION

Reflective behaviors, thoughts, and processes seem likely to occur most successfully in cultural institutions when several circumstances are present:

- The learner chooses the problem or the subject matter and controls the focus of attention.
- Using specific language, the learner creates and develops a question or a constellation of related questions.
- The questions involve a specific situation as it is present in an object or text; it is understood as an intellectual problem, with strands and contexts leading to related problems.
- These expanded contexts involve the exploration of differences, alternative perspectives, contrasting examples.
- Old ideas and assumptions are at risk; new frames for thought are possible.
- Documentation of the process is careful, leading to a useful record while conferring a narrative on the progress of the inquiry.
- Awareness of a design or pattern in the learner's process emerges during the pursuit of the inquiry.
- Awareness of applied practice as a thinker emerges in the learner; thinking in the cultural institution becomes a conscious skill.

When these or similarly constructive conditions are present in the museum or the library, the potential for chaos that often appears in the experience of the independent learner is reduced. Personal control and specificity of thought and language assist the learner to develop expanding repertoires and strategies for controlling and understanding information. The learner's consciousness of exploration and difference are likely to influence intellectual progress in a tentative mood. Literal documentation and attention to detail suggest a nearly repertorial stance; and in this sense, the learner can become a witness to his or her own intellectual emergence. Finally, the generative, connective qualities of information structures in libraries and museums easily lead to other structures elsewhere.

Ideally, useful acts of critical thought in situations of this kind will lead the learner beyond the limits of the immediate institution, to additional venues for inquiry. Over time, systematic explorations of cultural resources will broaden the individual's conceptual range, interweaving it more densely with other strands of knowledge and experience. The processes of museum or library use are adaptive and progressive, exploratory journeys that cross disciplines, leaving documented trails we can retrace. When faced with cognitive uncertainty in the future—How do I know this? Where did I learn it?—by looking back the learner can remember the contributions of those places where the most informing and firmly grounded options have been found.[32]

None of this comes easily. Even in an ideal world for learners, every thought that survives its instant lives against the odds. Acts of cognitive management and personal construction in cultural institutions constitute significant problem-solving events where the "tensions of consciousness" in Berger and Luckmann's phrase do not go away, but change form. Despite the power of the museum or the library to create enriched, nurturing situations for the development of personal knowledge, most of these settings are weak advocates for the learner. Suggestions or strategies for independent learning are generally missing; allusions to related concepts and contexts are unusual; the atmosphere for deliberate self-definition as a learner is rare. Even when librarians, curators, educators, and other professionals are present, independent learners in cultural institutions are rarely offered usable public models, lighted paths, or supportive advisors. In settings devoted to objects and texts, the articulation of processes is typically submerged, and the fate of the individual mind is barely illuminated. The tenacious, reflective learner—the critical thinker—often survives in defiance of disorder, technology, and noise.

CULTURAL INSTITUTIONS AS INSTRUMENTS FOR ADULT TRANSFORMATION

One definition of "critical" cited by Raymond Williams comes from its medical usage, "to refer to a turning point; hence decisive."[33] In this context the metaphor of the watershed may be used to emphasize museums and libraries—especially when they support critical thinking—as turning points for learners. Literally, a watershed is a divide, a high area of land that separates river systems from one another. On each side of the watershed, headwaters and rivers flow in opposite directions.[34] The cultural institution as a metaphoric watershed may be understood as a dividing line in an intellectual landscape or as a formative experience from which thinking flows differently. Experiences of critical thought in adult life contribute to the construction of a watershed when their effects assist transitions or transformations; that is, when they assist us to cross the various divides separating us from our maturity. The metaphor may resonate with Mezirow's description of "perspective transformation":

> The process of becoming critically aware of how and why our presuppositions have come to constrain the way we perceive, understand, and feel about our world; of reformulating these assumptions to permit a more inclusive, discriminating, permeable, and integrative perspective; and of making decisions or otherwise acting upon these new understandings. *More inclusive, discriminating, permeable, and integrative perspectives are superior perspectives* that adults choose if they can because they are motivated to better understand the meaning of their experience.[35] [Italics in original.]

Jerrold Apps describes a similar form of watershed experience as "emancipatory learning" based on multiple assumptions; among them,

> [t]hat human beings are free to act on their world; that human beings, differing from other living creatures, have the alternative of being able to create and modify their world; that they have the ability to reflect on their past, to be conscious of the present, and to make plans for the future; and that as persons work toward changing social structures and social situations, they themselves change.[36]

A useful description of cultural institutions as watershed institutions—settings for adult transformation and, in Apps's sense, emancipation from the structures of others—has ten elements.

1. Cultural institutions emphasize connections among disparate experiences and otherwise fragmented information.
2. They offer arrays of data and alternative paths toward these data.
3. Contextual information abounds.

4. The learner constructs order, structure, or pattern typically without interference; judgments are emergent, "provisional, relative, and contextual," not predetermined.[37]

5. Cultural institutions offer grounded, empirical, direct experiences of artifacts and texts; each experience acts upon expectations and changes them. In this way, as the psychologist George Kelly suggests, behavior itself can become a question.[38]

6. Cultural institutions nurture nonroutine, exploratory thoughts.

7. Because they concentrate stimuli and make them immediately available, museums and libraries are conducive to peak experiences.

8. Because they stimulate language, they are conducive to clarity and accuracy in perceptions; language makes classifications, questions, and judgments possible.

9. Cultural institutions have a particularly adult character: they match the reflective modes of age; they assist in distinctions between ideals and realities; they lead to renewal, or suggest the possibility of renewal; and they permit us to compare the past with the new.

10. They are conducive to self-directed change, movement not only beyond the information given, but movement beyond the self as given. It is possible to learn in the museum or the library that we are more capable, more perceptive, more interesting than we think.

This last is a particular challenge. If cultural institutions are ever going to be understood as educative, they must be prepared to cause a little trouble with people's ideas of themselves as learners.

HEURISTIC QUESTIONS FOR UNDERSTANDING CULTURAL INSTITUTIONS

The reader, poised since early in this essay at the brink of a great cultural institution, is now invited to enter as a critical thinker, a user, a learner, moving forward, minding what to do. The learner is also invited to consider the following heuristic for use in cultural institutions. This is a procedure for looking at the known and the unknown, and for finding ways to use the former to reduce the latter. We use tacit heuristic processes in most of the logical problem solving we do; it is important that we might use them more deliberately in the cultural institution. We can look at the arrangements and details of what we see in order to understand it. We can develop an approach to the problems and their contexts we perceive, based on what we already know and what we have done with similar problems in the past. We can carry out the approach as well as we can, according to the unknowns we are after, as well as we can understand them. Finally, we can look back and evaluate how well we have performed (in Iser's sense) the meanings of our new experiences.[39]

More specifically, critical approaches to cultural institutions might use some of the following questions. They are intended to address the information at hand, the need to devise and carry out a plan, and the need to look backward. Each question is intended to stimulate a response to immediate information and experience, and so to begin the processes of comprehending sensations and concepts. There are no correct answers to these questions—only exploratory responses, true to the feelings and senses.

What information and objects have been brought here? What ideas accompany them? How promising are these ideas in the light of my interests?

What is the situation for learning, and what constraints does it present? How will I recognize the difficult parts of this experience? How might I best approach these challenges? How might I best overcome these constraints?

What paths are open to me, where do I begin, and what is likely to follow? What essential are given? What is familiar to me? How is what I already know likely to be useful? What is expected of me here?

How have I behaved usefully in similar situations in the past? How will I know when I have found something useful or new? Is this what I expected to occur? What are my new questions now?

Polya says, "The aim of heuristic is to study the methods and rules of discovery and invention" through a form of "mental discourse."[40] A heuristic process, whatever form it takes, can be a systematic way to respond to hesitation, uncertainty, complexity, or challenge. It recognizes the need for tentative, experimental, even improvisational intellectual behavior. The heuristic tends to display and organize the learner's risk, mixing experiences, memories, and unknowns, helping the learner to construct an innovative life out of meanings based in memory—and then to go beyond the information given, toward the purely new.

It is always important to use naive questions whenever possible, and to keep them simple: What is going on here? What memories are brought to mind? How might I use them to move forward? Naive questions, assuming nothing, turn the inquirer into a stranger; they take away cultural knowledge and easy assumptions about museums and libraries. They subtract the element that obscures much of our lived reality, the taken-for-granted, the knowledge grounded in self-assurance alone. Their intention is to introduce a distance between the knower and knowledge. In doing so they lead to more specialized observations. "What is going on here?" is a broad, framing question. It seeks processes, behaviors, and patterns of communication in the cultural institution. "What memories are brought to mind?" leads directly to the personal constructions of a private life. "How might I use them to move forward?" may be the most important of all naive questions, because it looks ahead, leading to a critical stance in the presence of possibility.

Asking good questions about situations for learning can help the learner to become a critical designer of cognitive experiences outside schools. Perhaps they are usable guiding questions in the creation or the imagination of an educationally mindful life.

> What does this institution empower me to do with what I know?
> Does it offer me choices as I pursue my inquiry?
> Does it provide me with information or guidance to sharpen my perceptions?
> Does it provide me with a human being to answer my questions?
> Does it inquire about my expectations?
> Does it assist me to discover my own procedures, find my own way?
> Am I required to know something before I can find my own way?
> How am I to think of this experience?

Over time, the reality of learning in a cultural institution can be illuminated through observations stimulated by such questions. So can knowledge of what cultural institutions are, how they address their learners, and how they succeed or fail to live up to them. Questions are best defined in a phrase lifted from the critic I. A. Richards: "speculative instruments."[41] They are engines of language that move and direct attention in probing ways. Simple, naive questions start at the surface of things, but they soon yield to other more complex, deeper questions connected (as in a hall of slightly shifting mirrors) to other resonant reflections. These critical questions address the cultural institution interpreting itself as an informing environment. They ask how it nurtures its learners and informs their thoughts. They ask how the cultural institution thinks of itself, and embedded in that is how it thinks of the individual human being, practicing intelligence, learning on the edge.

NOTES

1. Peter L. Berger and Thomas Luckmann, *The Social Construction of Reality* (New York: Anchor, 1966), 21.

2. Berger and Luckmann, *Social Construction*, 25f.

3. Mihaly Csikszentmihalyi, *Beyond Boredom and Anxiety* (San Francisco: Jossey-Bass, 1977), 36.

4. John W. Gardner, *No Easy Victories* (New York: Harper, 1968), 32.

5. Ellen J. Langer, "Minding Matters: The Consequences of Mindlessness-Mindfulness," *Advances in Experimental Social Psychology* 22 (1989): 138–139.

6. Langer, "Minding Matters," 139.

7. Jack Mezirow, ed., *Fostering Critical Reflection in Adulthood: A Guide to Transformative and Emancipatory Learning* (San Francisco: Jossey-Bass, 1990), 15. See also Jack Mezirow, "A Critical Theory of Self-Directed Learning," in *Self Directed-Learning: From Theory to Practice*, ed. Stephen Brookfield (San Francisco: Jossey-Bass, New Directions for Continuing Education, no. 25, 1985).

8. Mezirow, *Fostering Critical Reflection*, 6–9.

9. Mezirow, *Fostering Critical Reflection*, 9.

10. Mezirow, *Fostering Critical Reflection*, 8.

11. See Stephen D. Brookfield, *Developing Critical Thinkers* (San Francisco: Jossey-Bass, 1987); Matthew Lipman, *Critical Thinking: What Can It Be?* (Upper Montclair, NJ: Montclair State College, Institute for Critical Thinking, Resource Publication Series 1, no. 1, 1988); Richard Paul, *Two Conflicting Theories of Knowledge, Learning and Literacy: The Didactic and the Critical* (Upper Montclair, NJ: Montclair State College, Institute for Critical Thinking, Resource Publication Series 1, no. 2, 1988).

12. Paul, *Two Conflicting Theories*, 6.

13. Brookfield, *Developing Critical Thinkers*, 5.

14. Maxine Greene, "In Search of a Critical Pedagogy," *Harvard Educational Review* 56, no. 4 (November 1986): 438.

15. See Maxine Greene, "Education and the Public Space," *Educational Researcher* 11, no. 6 (June–July 1982): 4–9; Maxine Greene, *Dialectic of Freedom* (New York: Teachers College Press, 1988).

16. Ronald Lee Fleming et al., "Whatever Became of the Public Square?" *Harper's* 281, no. 1682 (July 1990): 58–59.

17. See Jerome S. Bruner, "Going Beyond the Information Given," in *Beyond the Information Given*, ed. Jeremy M. Anglin (New York: Norton, 1973), 218–238.

18. Jerome S. Bruner, "Art as a Mode of Knowing," in *On Knowing: Essays for the Left Hand* (New York: Atheneum, 1965), 68.

19. Bruner, "Art," 70.

20. Bruner, "Art," 72–73.

21. Mihaly Csikszentmihalyi, *Flow: The Psychology of Optimal Experience* (New York: Harper and Row, 1990), 69.

22. Maxine Greene, "The Art of Being Present: Education for Aesthetic Encounters," *Journal of Education* 166, no. 2: 133–134.

23. John Seely Brown, Allan Collins, and Paul Duguid, "Situated Cognition and the Culture of Learning," *Educational Researcher* 18, no. 1 (January–February 1989): 32.

24. Brown, Collins, and Duguid, "Situated Cognition," 33.

25. Brown, Collins, and Duguid, "Situated Cognition," 34.

26. Langer, "Minding Matters," 150–151.

27. Wolfgang Iser, *The Act of Reading* (Baltimore: Johns Hopkins Press, 1978), 27.

28. Jerome S. Bruner, *Actual Minds, Possible Worlds* (Cambridge: Harvard University Press, 1986), 34.

29. Bruner, *Actual Minds,* 122.

30. Mezirow, *Fostering Critical Reflection in Adulthood,* 354.

31. Csikszentmihalyi, *Flow,* 217.

32. Ellen J. Langer, *Mindfulness* (Reading, MA: Addison-Wesley, 1989), 143.

33. Raymond Williams, *Keywords,* rev. ed. (New York: Oxford University Press, 1983), 85.

34. *World Book Encyclopedia,* 1978 ed., s.v. "divide."

35. Mezirow, *Fostering Critical Reflection in Adulthood,* 14.

36. Jerrold Apps, *Improving Practice in Continuing Education* (San Francisco: Jossey-Bass, 1985), 153.

37. Brookfield, *Developing Critical Thinkers,* 17.

38. George A. Kelly, "Behaviour as an Experiment," in *Perspectives in Personal Construct Theory,* ed. D. Bannister (London: Academic Press, 1970), 260–261.

39. Derived from G. Polya, *How to Solve It,* 2nd ed. (Princeton: Princeton University Press, 1957).

40. Polya, *How to Solve It,* 112, 133.

41. I. A. Richards, *Speculative Instruments* (London: Routledge & Kegan Paul, 1955).

2

WHAT I SAW IN THE MUSEUM

Twenty years ago I went to the museum and my living world changed. I saw an array of objects and texts, and another array, and another, and another, each of them connective and promising. Each collection invited that part of my mind capable—increasingly capable, I found—of resonance and extension. The museums I saw informed me of an entirely new stratum of motive and implication among institutions and collections: I often sensed an invitational voice, almost a calling out.

What I saw in the museum, what I sensed, was an inviting structure, held in place by inferences and implications, ideas and concepts, suggestions of the possible. However deeply I looked, there was always something beyond, something I had not seen yet. I learned that, by paying attention, writing and photographing, I could repossess these moments of anticipation and promise at any time; the open invitation was never withdrawn. Twenty years on, it still holds my attention. Yet my learning remains at best partial, incomplete, and inarticulate.

I have held museums in mind over the whole of my life; yet so diverse and pervasive are their traces—and so personal are my responses—that I cannot recover them justly or fully. My memory, energy, and promise failed me often, still it was proven everywhere I looked: all inquiry is generative, connective, and therefore potentially infinite.

I tried to write, to capture it all. I made my notes, observing through the smallest windows of chance and circumstance, striving and wanting to see. Only one idea became clear: in these places I found the strands of a cognitive fabric waiting for me, the weaver. It still waits, unfinished; it always will wait.

The museum offered me an invitation to leave the momentum of one life and enter times and spaces set apart, where I saw a different worldliness, and felt a different momentum. This difference mattered, and it became my guiding unknown. I was invited to see a new, more whole reflection of the fragmented world. The museum redefined my experiences in order for me to do my work, which I came to see as everyone's work: renegotiating a fair and new understanding among frail and easily broken assumptions that, when challenged, lead us to learn.

The museum offered a confusion that was also an enticement, even a seduction. I saw an object bathed and illuminated, seemingly unpossessed, as at times I have wanted to see and touch the textures of living skin. I entered this illuminated world as much by the chaos in my senses as by the logic. Always alone, I found these sensations to be the exquisite transport out of solitude I required.

The beginnings of these encounters were inevitably based on what I saw, what I felt within, and what surrounded me; the visual and the architectural often implied a promise that opened my senses wide. I walked forward then as a moving, more feeling system, made ready for some unknown, but open and fearless. These physical places invited me to trust myself at once as I entered what I came to think of as the possible world.

I also came to see the idea of the open, inviting door as a definitive image in a free culture. To me the door implied a vocabulary of open practice, conversational, tentative: enter, feel, then observe and respond, then question. It became certain to me that, given a fair opportunity and useful information, intelligence can happen in the world. My task was to let intelligence happen in myself, and to observe its growth. Tacit conversations I held with material objects led me to make moves and take risks, look again, think again. My moves led me to observe, my observations led me to reflect, my reflections led to me to feel engaged by what might happen next. I found my practice in an institution's open values and not the closed; I found my intelligence to require an open way.

I was rarely challenged to ask my own questions, except by myself. I could easily have been invited to imagine and create the open door. Instead I was given the answers to many questions I had not asked or even considered. But I learned to cultivate the attentions and energies of an open practice for myself, building an unguarded, receptive approach as I walked among other users. I wrote more. I added my human voice to counter the other voices. I observed my own immersion. My experiences were at times so private and deeply personal that I felt challenged to find words. I found that experience without conversation is deprivation: and so, much of what I saw in the museum, the full array of associations and systems evoked by my progress, cannot be recovered, having been unspoken.

Given a path toward the open door, an invited mind will race to reach it. The door became an essential metaphor to me, even a precise characteristic, of democratic experience. What do I see here? What am I to make of this? Where is the open door? The first thing a collection tacitly promised was that I could come to know something new, and therefore could become someone new, because I had arrived here as a learner, where something essential and fresh awaited me. This is what I told myself could happen.

I found that even the best collection is about what is missing. I wanted to grasp the movements of long-dead hands. *How did she do that?* I tried to imagine Darwin's processes of mind. *How did he think that?* To hear the sounds of Cro-Magnon music. *A flute of bone?* To "know" or "understand" the traces of squalor in Theresienstadt. *How can this be "understood"?* I encountered only traces. I left each collection thinking of what had disappeared. As museums became more about the missing concept—and as my experiences of collections intensified—the museum in the mind became less dependent on vision, and more dependent on thought.

And so: an object invited me to consider its visible character, its situation, the surrounding space, and also the shadow of what was not there, the trace of what had disappeared. Nothing visible has meaning without the nearness of something invisible. We are given to see what this thing is, intact, presented before us. We are given to understand what we are able to recover for ourselves from the invisible patterns we fabricate and hold within.

I draw myself to the Cycladic figure, among my first objects as a museum user. Then and now it moves me to imagine its creation and survival, carrying ages later the energy of an irrecoverable origin. Within the object, something is moving. It comes from somewhere beyond us, from some place we are unlikely to have seen. Then it is nearby. Then it is before us. Then it is gone. I see the thing, feel its energy, see the moving shadow. There is a whisper that reveals the object as an idea. There is an archaeology of human motive and intention in the object. I am required to consider it, to search for the right word to say. My tentative articulation of what I have seen is a form of excavation, and also a form of filling in. My experience remains an artifact of coincidence, memory, and the occasionally brave idea.

We do not grow or learn by going *to* something, we learn by going *through* something. For me, the museums became a continuous passage; I moved through it from experience to experience. We enter museums to enter ourselves; we come to entrance ourselves. The museum is the performance of my meanings, my observations and reflections on memories; it is also the path that will open when I leave the museum. A museum remains perpetually incomplete because it implies the idea of elsewhere. There is no meaning independent of the contexts we can imagine and hold as our own, and yet these can become resonant and infinite.

I think there is a moment when a museum has not yet begun for me, when it is entirely ideal and entirely possible to grasp fully every object, every idea. This moment occurs as I enter, rushing greedily to see, and so to possess, it all. But the possessive moment disappears instantly when I want to keep it forever, leaving nothing to possess except what I think of it. There is another moment afterward in reflection, when the museum is over for me, but I am filled by it. Inevitably, I have wanted too much. I want too much still.

There are many possibilities of experience in the invitational institution: we absorb, hold, assemble, connect, construct; we fabricate; we plan, we expect, we anticipate, we hope; we hypothesize, infer, assume, fantasize; we ask, pause, converse, clarify, return and linger, compare, elaborate, recollect; we remember and evoke; we discover and surrender, we become. We thread the needle of our thought, and then we sew. We wait; we want. And as we do, we stitch the fabric of experience.

Twenty years, and still the museum and its user await each other; the museum and its user await the imaginations of each other until they meet.

3

WHAT I READ IN THE LIBRARY

These are my themes: community, memory, trust, knowledge, help, and fearlessness. We would not live in a place where none of these things is present because we will find them to be the essential elements of a culture of stories. Nor would we live where there is ignorance, or an overlaying climate of hesitation, or cynicism, or venality, or the seamless fabric of the false. When we find these things in our world, we turn toward the authentic, for strength and energy; we look into nearby lived lives and experiences, for the evidence of humanity; and we also turn toward each other for models of how to live, how to be calm and unafraid of change.

If we did not have these things in our lives, we would want them, and we would do our best to create them. We would strive to find human qualities of thought and kindness, a combination of intelligence and fearlessness, to lead us in finding our way toward truths we need to craft. We would want a vision of what is possible for us, so small in a world so large. We would need a sense of order and structure, because a progressive life requires us to weave together many goals and many hopes—and for the strength of this fabric we will turn to each other.

And when we turn to each other that is when the stories appear: we need to keep mindful of where we began and how our evolution is going, so far. We need to know the lessons learned, the signs we have interpreted along the way, the events that made us feel strong, or ashamed, or powerless, or misunderstood; we need to know the ways we have to shape the future as more than a series of accidents and heartbreaks. And those events we still cannot understand will represent to us the knowledge we need to gather in order to live, and the mysteries we will be telling as we make a community's safe place out of emptiness. We would not live without these things or the processes of thinking that surround them. We would not live without a library.

At first I was drawn to the library because I could neither trust nor ethically participate in schools as a teacher. Against all the constraints and damage I saw in schools, the thoughts that led me forward allowed me to envision an infinite conversation, in progress every day I worked with people and information. Information has always been a process and not a thing to me: it resists management and reduction, it wants to be connected to other information, it needs to be lived as an experience of change. My work in libraries informed my life and helped it to be transformed; gradually I was able to express what I saw the library to be. It is not a place to *keep* things but to *hold* them until they can be given away; not a place but a process, a making of something new for a common life.

I came to see that knowledge makes a person's life exactly as it makes the life of a community: knowledge assists both the person and the community to emerge from crisis and to discover continuity and possibility. In everyday exchanges and civilities in a fair and open place, we acknowledge that we are equal occupants within it. What we know about ourselves and what we feel within the library makes it our place. What we do in it, what we may build or provide here, makes it into an engine of connection to others in a larger world. Knowledge, not an economy, makes a community, even if it is the story of flaws and failures, or if its sum is a record of departures and impermanence. What we must love most about our libraries and our communities is neither their outcomes nor their achievements, but the ways they have of making people smart and connected and safe. When institutions and communities do not do this for themselves, they will always fail.

Communities are foremost deep mines of knowing. Knowledge constructs a community by moving from person to person and from generation to generation. We transmit our ways of doing things, and our ways of seeing things from here; we remind ourselves of great changes in time, and the gradual, forestlike evolution of our culture. When knowledge allows our community to become broader, more inclusive, and more open, our way of speaking and understanding also grows more capable of expressing shared integrity and mutual respect.

Every life teaches, every life is a lesson, but every life needs a voice and a place. We become stronger when we speak about our lives; our thoughts become more connected and more resonant simultaneously. Our strengths come slowly over time, but our discoveries and insights can strike us like lightning, each one giving us a surge and a promise. Most people will also find courage, trust, and empathy in themselves as they find knowledge, and as they think among others. We may learn the condition of the world as it is, but every learning also has an implication for what it might become, and what we might know next about it.

If we are a community, information and complexity will nourish and awaken us. Challenges will define our ethics and character. If we are learners, our conflicts require us to become stronger and more resilient; differences among us engage both our conscience and our spine. If we are a community, we engage in civic discourse, conversations about how we expect the world to be, and how we can wrestle with it toward the better.

We are given this task: to live up to the challenges of knowing everything we can where we are, and then to go beyond it, to make something greater of it, and to make something more of ourselves through it. Our task is to know, and to express, as much as we can, and to listen with care.

I think that these things are true: Every opportunity people have to gather information and establish a fair point of view (as they can in libraries) will nourish their consideration, ethics, and conscience. The weaving together of our many-stranded experiences into a community narrative (as occurs in libraries) strengthens our responsibility to others. As information and complexity increase (in accord with the purposes of libraries), the likelihood of understanding entire patterns of life increases as well.

The library and the museum are the only institutions in our culture capable of continuously opening the closed doors of memory and indifference. These institutions compose a form of mind for our culture that is always fluid, expanding to contain the emerging flow of thought and possibility. They are capable as well of returning us constantly to the unfinished issues we carry with us as a culture.

As I think of unfinished issues, I mean our failure, or inability, or fear to engage in essential conversations about the unspoken themes of human lives, and the need for respect and generosity in our assumptions about each other. Among our unfinished issues, I would include our great cultural losses: the world that is shy of poetry, the missing lessons of history and memory, and the disappearance of conversations that last into the night. I would include as well the endangered conscience.

When we have reduced everything that requires reflection and conversation to nothing, not even whispered conversations, how shall we become ourselves? How shall we become our own persons under constraints of narrow entertainment and anti-intellectualism? People need to be able to see themselves woven into the tapestry of their times, not view their lives on screens, or stand outside them as visitors, audiences, or victims. As we encounter surrogates for reality or imagination or pleasure or thought, how do we live a life we can trust to be our own? It has taken me years to begin this for myself, and it is why I stand up for libraries.

Libraries remind us that knowledge is a living process that moves us forward. But the library we enter today also embodies a backbone in our civic lives—an essential place that will always resist the simplification, reduction, and insipid superficiality that frequently characterizes contemporary information. Schooling and media do not help us to do this; their task is to mask authenticity. Books and information alone cannot accomplish this, because a cultural narrative can appear only when living people and their memories are present together.

Libraries collect lives and the traces of lives. Libraries document connections between lives, and the gathering of lives for causes, or celebrations, or for civic duties, or for wars. Libraries keep track of the rising and falling of wealth and power in lives. They gather the evidences of genius, invention, and failure; they record the lives of artists and apprentices. Like naturalists, they keep their eyes on the living system of the community: on its geography and intellectual climate, its systems of balance and relationship, on the order of its living contexts, on all living things here in our small sphere. Libraries capture the migrations of knowledge and the changes left behind in traces and dust.

When we look at the records we have made, we can know certain lessons. Our experiences today are infinite, because they resonate and mirror the experiences of the past. We may find that all heroes have a bit of tarnish and that all greatness has a stripe of venality. We may find that in history it is often the smallest players whose stories tell us the most. Knowledge nurtures what we think of the possibilities of life. To know more means that our possibilities grow.

Every day librarians live one life in a shared world of individual lives. Every day they live with the unfinished issues and lives of other human beings, and with the acts of giving that compose a life of service. They practice the critical acts of giving in the words they say to people who live amid change and need, and in the ways they live up to their instincts for generosity. Hardware may do the work, but software—helping words and generous attention—lasts a longer time. There is nothing that can replace the question librarians ask of every library user: What is the bridge you need to build with my help?

We become who we are meant to be through thinking, reading, and writing, speaking with others, and giving our attention to what we believe in. We work in a fluid information environment that surrounds us every day, where our engagements with *processes* (and not things) are about as certain as we can be. Neither professional mastery nor professional identity is ever fixed. This is a good condition of life: in the face of new unknowns every day, to learn who we are and what we are capable of doing never ends. Otherwise, how much of ourselves would be lost beyond rescue? How differently would we have to live without our trust and experience in this place?

We want to move forward to embrace our own lives, but safely and fearlessly; we want to shape our own becoming among people in a place we can trust.

We are given tasks and crises by our lives; we learn to assume responsibility for knowledge, and we create our strength in response.

We build a human world that has never been built before, and never will be finished.

We find that the steady tensions of one life, each life's compelling issues, keep us in a state of unease and lead us on.

We believe that the experience of living permits us to possess something that does not disappear.

We are all held together in a fabric of stories; we are enriched by the possibilities of interpretation; and we are made strong by acts of helping each other to listen.

We want a life that has the qualities of wholeness and integrity; and at its center, we want there to be a fire.

What we find in the library is the fire inside ourselves.

4

WANTING, AT TEN

Perhaps people trust museums because they associate them with a time in their lives when the compromises and conditions of living had not yet revised their shallow but confident expectations. Museums may be trusted, and they may be trustworthy, but we should be clear: if our institutions are trusted for the wrong reasons—because they hold the truth, the facts, the relics of patriotism—it is not a blessing.[1] Shallow trust places museums at a loss; it misses their complexity, and dulls the edge of their integrity. That edge has to be sharp and clear or no one learns. Perhaps museums want to be trusted every day, but some days it may be better to hone the museum's edge by risking the safety of the place. I remind myself that cultural institutions are revolutionary structures; they only appear to be safe.

Museum users may trust that the museum offers the authentic, the grounded, even the coherent. Museum users may trust that, for a moment in the museum, ambiguity is held at bay. But the museum voice that offers the user a soothing and uncomplicated truth puts its purpose at risk. Some days, if the museum is really to live up to its purpose, that voice will provoke wariness and caution, make a small incision of provocation, or plant a viable seedling of doubt. Some days, the museum will want to remind its users that it is for their thinking, and not their trust, that they are wanted here. Some days, the museum might set fire to the museum map in the user's hand; heat, light, and disquiet are essential to what is done here.

All cultural institutions need to be kept at the edge of their integrity each day, but for the right reasons. I still search for the incendiary museum, the museum that stirs conventions and excites risks, because it is risk at the edges of lived experience that illuminates the possible. Possibilities are the business of cultural institutions, but only if the institutions are trusted *because* they challenge and incite in ways that lead the edge of knowledge forward for many users. In the name of the user, museums need to challenge convention and take public risks for experience, learning, and change.

The more we risk, the more we learn. A museum restores the Enola Gay, a principal emblem of the twentieth century, and the object with its given texts reinvigorates and then unfortunately reifies the differences between experience and history. Important communication between scholarship and experience do not occur as they might have. Could the risk of an open conversation have occurred? Could human interpretive differences, unresolved as ever, have become part of the public's understanding of how history works?

The more we risk, the more we learn. A museum displays the photographs of a modern master, just dead of AIDS, and the city places its director on trial. By some accounts, no work of controversial art has appeared in the city since then. Was it possible to educate that city, to address the risk of art and the certainty of fear *through* the museum, instead of against it? Threatened, fearful people—morally guided, but sometimes dictatorial and uncompromising—can commandeer the public mind and prevent the conversations we require if we are to fully understand our time.

But then some wonderful thing can happen; a structure is created that compels us not to turn away from a hard recognition. The American record of human losses in Vietnam is etched in stone on the National Mall in our capital city, and when the abstract ideal of memory and patriotic death is altered in this way, the nation is seared by its vision, and knows its experience anew and in a different light. Without compromising the power of loss, the courageous memorial provides a missing language and its voice, spoken only there, in the presence of black granite. What lessons are present as well? What clarities of thinking and feeling are evoked without one didactic word? How many stories have these edges, and when we encounter them, what causes our trust as we approach them?

In lower Manhattan, at Battery Park, the Museum of Jewish Heritage, a memorial to the Holocaust opens, to tell more than the story of ineradicable horrors—to give to this dreadful history the treasure of context and detail through human voices and experiences. The user proceeds through a narrative from vibrant cultural life, through devastation and loss, to renewal and remembrance. Without a moment of compromise, the strands of narrative restore the vitality, rather than the vulnerability alone, of a scarred but surviving and self-renewing people. History remains unchanged, and the museum user is bereft, but understands far more than grief.

Given a fair chance, in an environment of humility and sincere inquiry, smart and open people can learn to accept the challenges of an institution to think and feel independently. The cultural institution must craft its assumptions carefully as it addresses difficult human experiences. There is an arrogance to knowledge, we must remember, and so we need to assure that we remain open to alternative experiences to our own, open to the possible learning that only museums can create, even for those who are immersed in the museum's curriculum. That curriculum at times can be opaque and unquestioned; it is one way that museums can be much like public schools.

Trust matters most when we are afraid, when life seems to be largely constructed of difficult questions and harsh expectations, and when we are working to resolve our feelings. Risk is by definition unwanted and undesirable in most parts of our lives; and also unwanted are people like me who say hooray for risk, bring risk on, because we believe that no one learns or changes without daring, no one changes without risking something, taking action against the odds. This is a theme of trust and the necessity of risk: trust makes risk possible, and therefore makes learning possible. Risking ourselves is the only way we have to design and renew ourselves, and to take responsibility for our own intellectual lives.

Therefore, the task in museums and libraries, if they wish to be regarded with authentic trust by diverse citizens, is to construct situations for authentic risking and questioning. This is a value that binds citizens and institutions. Cultural institutions are places to avow and advocate fearless self-knowledge as the essential preliminary condition for a life of both risk and trust.

Inquiry requires people to open themselves. Read something, discuss something, and a new space (both literal and cognitive) is created for us to occupy, inhabited by the new, the alternative, or the unknown. Grounded within ourselves when we stand in conversation with others, the new cognitive space is like a room suddenly missing a wall. Trust is the management of courage and fear in the presence of risk. It is required for the courage to think.

Cultural institutions need to inspire trust so the learner can experience risk and yet also experience cognitive change without feeling devastating fear. We should speak of trust as the animating force that, through the thinking institution, moves into the user, infusing its energy at the critical moments of lived experience. As we contemplate the museum, each of us needs to speak as a learner among learners, a participant who anticipates a surge of energy and will. I first knew that energy when I was ten, long before I was lost (as I remain today) in the mistrust and anxiety of adulthood.

As I wrote those words the thought occurred to me that, at ten, I may have been the best I will ever be at practicing that great museum quality, wanting. I wanted so much! Now, as I reread my adult museum diaries, I find a different kind of strong wanting that has brought me to this place. But at ten, I wanted so much to be a person of integrity—an *adult* person of integrity—a person with more certainty than fear about himself, a person who hoped to be less isolated and less afraid than he would ever in fact be. It has been an apprehensive life, except for that brief time. What I wanted, an adult competence I could feel was truly mine, has never fully come to me. There has always been more fear than certainty. But at ten I knew courage and curiosity, and I hoped for more to happen than actually did. I knew trust in myself as a learner, and I thought it would never leave me.

Fifty years later, here is what I know about institutions and trust.

No one should trust an institution that does not reveal itself. Therefore an institution should make itself transparent.

No one should trust an institution that speaks only to itself. Therefore an institution should speak widely among other institutions, and to its users.

No one should trust an institution that does not acknowledge experiences outside itself. Therefore an institution should connect to the lived experiences and memories that construct contemporary life.

No one should trust an institution that has no room for reflection. Therefore an institution should ask questions it cannot answer out loud, making them the signature questions of the institution.

No one should trust an institution that does not learn. Therefore an institution should ask more, listen more, reflect more, document more.

No one should have to feel alone as a learner.

To evoke trust we need to understand and express context, the core of authenticity. Context, by which I mean not the tree but the soil, not the fish but the water, not the person but the family, not the concept but the mind on fire.

When we set out to do what we do, to help people to change themselves in the presence of new information, contexts must be apparent for trust to happen. In contrast, mystery and awe are forms of entertaining incoherence, facts and events without contexts; they hold the possibility of confusion and failure. If awe and mystery are extensive and pervasive, they will thwart trust and progress for the learner. An open fabric of contexts and connections is what matters most for thought and growth. In this contextual transparency and generative evidence, an institution is proven to be great.

Mystery is different from promise, and it is different from possibility. Mystery is a body in a closed room. In any place for learning, needless mystery and arrogant expertise taunt and mock the user; they make possibility more distant, not less.

Context, generosity, and kindness generate trust. People must be helped generously, if they are to develop new awareness. A learner needs open expectations, understanding that something more is possible to learn. Cultural institutions should build trust on this: our *knowledge* is incomplete; our *understanding* of what we know is even less complete; but our *capacity* for grasping connections in the world is great and undeveloped. There are always alternatives to our own thoughts: this is true for everyone. We are always capable of finding more. Learners are works in progress, all of us improvising our construction of trust every day.

I have simple advice; at least it sounds simple. I sometimes find it useful to remind myself that, in cultural institutions, libraries, or museums, the place completes nothing. We have the easy work: we plan, name, display, evaluate, reach outward. Our tasks are to make connections visible, to make complexities inviting, to understand possible further connections, and to demonstrate every day how unfinished and incomplete, and yet how driven by context our knowledge is. It is the user who works to complete the circle (if it can be completed), who strives to make an experience relevant and useful, and who carries an idea beyond the immediate moment of experience into the lived world. Our reminder to ourselves must be steady: think always with the user, know where the user is.

Trust is grounded on processes that are freely given and not withheld, that describe and demystify. We grow through processes that welcome thinking. As a teacher I have found that trust follows reciprocity: one gift engenders another. Trust is a consequence of something: an act, an utterance, an acceptance. What is the opposite of trust? Fear. What is the consequence of trust? Risk. What is the enemy of trust? Arrogance. What is the agent of trust? Generosity.

Hope is the imagination of the possible. Trust is the imagination that the possible is not beyond us, and will in fact happen. A learning life is constructed by hope and trust. We imagine ourselves growing through such possibilities. Two ideas or memories become confluent; someone speaks the word that has been missing from our understanding; an object, without moving, or making a sound, communicates some bold truth to us. A moment of insight does not emerge from memory, or from prior experience, or even from the brilliance of the object before us. It emerges from the situation created for something new to happen to us.

We may understand the presence of something that cannot be fully explained, something that almost escapes us.

We come to understand the tensions between the private and the public meanings of things.

We see differences between objects, and know that differences are meanings.

We learn to hold multiple ideas at once and recognize truths in each.

We experience the ancient and the contemporary and the timeless, in one thing.

We recognize the unfinished, an unclosing openness, in ourselves.

I place myself among others as a man who has lived fearfully for his entire life, even though as an educator I say it is better to be hopeful than to be fearful; even under threat we learn from hope, only hope. The genius of the museum lies in a fair chance to grasp the possible and leave behind our fears. Yet I think I will never be fearless enough to learn what I most need to learn or to change as fully as I must. I will never read or see enough. Now that I have passed sixty, I see I am still a wanting boy of ten, trying to grow. I encounter the unknown among objects continuously. I feel the tensions of information and intervention. I am an adult, and so I know that there is no single truth for me.

But I am also ten, and I am grateful that I can find in the museum the traces of possibility and devotion, the record of knowledge and continuity that promises so much. There is the intimacy and the privacy I need to begin and sustain my hopeful life. Someone unseen has created these worlds, these dream worlds, for my inspiration. The world is so generous here, so brilliant and open to my thinking. I am not fearful or worthless here, not a winner or a loser, neither right nor wrong. I am here to become. I am ready to work and risk, ready to read and think. I am ten.

We are all, perhaps, some part of us, ten and wanting; and the museum challenges us to live fully, to explore widely, and to love the art of knowing deeply. We are not able to say it, because we are ten, but here we discover the solace and strength that will come in the future from some possible selfless devotion to something we want to know, something beyond ourselves and our small world of knowledge, if only we can sustain it and trust ourselves to know more. At ten, we do not yet know how difficult it will be to sustain our attention, our mindfulness and devotion. Speaking for myself at ten, I did not know that there would be so much to fear, or so many losses, or so many ways every day to encounter one's own heart and mind.

Speaking of fear, perhaps we trust museums because they are not schools, and we know what schools have done both to us and for us. I am grateful for my education, but I am also grateful that museums do not diminish or classify or disrespect the individual life. They help us to understand and feel passion—not hide it—to understand and feel at once. It is this integrity, this simultaneous knowing and feeling, that drives whatever and whomever we are meant to be.

Now we live in thrall to mechanization, digitization, mediation, and micromanagement. I am a man of low expectations, pleased when the mail arrives, the plane lands safely, my vote is counted, my students speak. Each becomes a small way to revive hope in myself and trust in others. We are encouraged to trust by small acts as much as by enormous acts, but I think it is the smallest ones that matter most. They remind us that kindness has immense value and that the grace of generosity comes to us against the odds.

In museums and libraries, the acts that most inspire trust are those that stand against the miniaturization of the individual life and the cold storage of the heart. Through the experiences, examples, and thoughts that trace the history of our feelings, we restore and rescue ourselves by striving to understand all that has happened to us since we were ten.

NOTE

1. The American Association of Museums reported in 2004 that "[a]lmost nine out of ten Americans (87 percent) find museums to be one of the most trustworthy or a trustworthy source of information among a wide range of choices. Books are a distant second at 61 percent, and a majority of Americans find print and broadcast media and the Internet to be not trustworthy." Among the key findings of the survey is this: "The public's trust in museums is based on three themes: they present history, they are research-oriented, and they deal in facts." Museum Association of New York, "Americans Identify Museums as a Source of Information They Can Really Trust," <http://www.manyonline.org/AmericansTrust.htm> (18 October 2004).

5

RESCUING THE USER

THE LIFE LINE

Winslow Homer's 1884 painting "The Life Line"—at the Museum of Art in Philadelphia—is an emblem for the work of any contemporary cultural institution. Each of us holds on tightly to the continuity and experience that means our life, as chaos eddies just below, a brief descent away. Even without a shipwreck and a roaring storm, we often know that fragile passages are our essential journeys to make, if we want to continue and grow. It is our great need at those times for a lifeline, yes, but even more for a human being who is there to urge us forward with questions that evoke our hidden strength. Ideas of such trust and service, and hidden strengths, and the idea of rescue itself, have moved me forward all of my professional life.

My work is to create circumstances where cognitive bridges can be built among objects, among texts, moment to moment, mind to mind. These bridges are for human lives to cross, at times with trepidation. When we build them we participate in a human design, and we add both our grasp and our hope to its complexity and construction as we do. When we cross them, we strengthen them as possibilities for others and for our own future self-rescue.

Rescuing the user follows from the idea that the content of any cultural institution, when combined with the complexities and memories of one life, can evoke deeply affecting feelings, illuminate difficult unknowns, and open doors on experiences long closed or never before understood. Where do we turn when we need to understand something we have never seen before? To memory, to experience, to the unfinished parts of our educations, and sometimes to the chaos within. We nurture the hopes we have

43

for learning more. We turn to others as models, as agents, as helpers and companions. We also turn to others for rescue from the surrounding mindless undertow.

Cultural institutions hold uncountable, evanescent moments when the user stands in need of a word, a guide, or a path toward knowing something new. We need to remember how to remember at these moments; at such moments it is useful to think with another person.

Perhaps it is easy to see the importance of that idea in the case of an individual museum user, trying to figure out the motives and inspirations of abstract expressionism or the Native American spirit world, or in the case of a young library user amazed among atlases and world history reference tools. But I like to remind myself that cultural institutions are grounded not only on the mysteries they hold, but also in the evident strengths of their communities. Museums and libraries are human agencies for change; therefore it is from a common place among others that we might expect to find help.

Just as they cause the individual user to reach for something, cultural institutions also cause their communities to reach toward something that is mutual—something they are looking for but may be unable to describe, something that may transform them profoundly in ways they will not even notice. I think this reaching is the common human value of the place where selves are found; one part of this reaching is for rescue from isolation and thoughtlessness.

Museums cannot create a community or a culture, nor can libraries. But it is within the power of cultural institutions to lead users *toward* the invisible structures of knowledge and community: toward compassion and kindness, and through these two, toward grace (that is, generosity of spirit) and survival, and on to knowledge and intelligence. If over our life spans we are moved toward something larger than our lives, I believe we have to journey there by deliberately thinking ourselves forward among others, even though we may have different ideas of our destinations and be unaware of what we will find eventually. We are guided by forces we feel but cannot see; they move us together and toward something we might see but cannot feel.

In places like these we can practice the ability to give our attention for long periods of time; we think here. We are drawn to being here, and learning here, by passion and desire; here we want to make something happen for ourselves. This is evident in our continuous questions, and in the rhythms and patterns of the world as we sense it. I think that a person who comes to such places wants to be moved toward a palpable renewal of life. Here people can envision more clearly the people they are capable of becoming by asking their own questions. What people need most in this challenging place is a helping mind when feelings are in motion, or when expectations have been overturned, or when the sense of who we are has become unmoored.[1]

Only human beings can live out the complex plans of self-renewal and aspiration that require the energies of learning; human beings can become different by choice and practice. We can revise ourselves, think about something we want to understand, carry it with us for many years, and find small pieces of data, information, insight, and knowledge every time we enter a museum, a library, or a bookstore. We are moved to act on those things we feel to be most valuable to us.

We are anchored in lived experiences, and we will always be inspired to reinterpret them as we grow older and our perspectives become more complex. How many of us have thought of something that happened in high school, in our childhood family, in our neighborhoods, and come to it with a new insight? How many of us have thought today, or yesterday, of someone who has died or otherwise disappeared from our lives, yet whose sound of voice or gentle gesture is embedded every day in us? Knowledge, too, is embedded in this way and infused in our assumptions and questions.

We cannot close the door on our losses and our memories, or on our dearest knowledge. They are there in us; to think of them and want to understand them are acts of *human* being. We are not finished with our gains and losses, our curiosities, our connections, or our ideas yet. What has been given to us to make us human is endurance, our urge for integrity and understanding. In recent years our hearts have been especially full with that question, asked from hope, pain, and astonishment: *What does it mean to be a human being?* What does it mean that, when we have been feeling unmoored for some time, we come to the words and images of our lives in order to remember and restore ourselves, and to reach toward others?

What can happen when we speak directly to people about who they are, where they have come from, what they have brought here, what they remember, where they want to go, and what it is they see when they look into the mirror of their questions? The user needs a helping mind, an advocate for learning more, for exploring without fear, and for combining and connecting experiences. These are vital acts in the lives of people in cultural institutions, ways of rescue from experience without feeling. Every work in a collection can hold an evocative moment for someone: something there is intangibly present and moving, just for them. How can we pursue it? How can we make it more important to us, rather than allow the moment drift away, unkept? How do we rescue the user at that moment?

Cultural institutions are similar in that they are places where useful tensions occur, where play and work are connected, where we can encounter the conventional and (sometimes right next to it) the revolutionary. Here learners construct and build their own minds, for themselves. The learning is connective and integrative, often evolving slowly, over time, and not to be pursued as if for an examination. Here learners do not have to wait to receive the mind of a professor or other teacher; they combine pieces for themselves. But none of this is easy, even though it simply requires that we open our eyes and minds as widely as we can and follow what we see.

THE RESCUE

I encourage every educator, advocate, librarian, or guide in a cultural institution to think of how useful experiences will rescue the user. In order to make great experiences happen between people, to remove the masks that often hide us in libraries and museums, and to make the risks of learning less daunting and more possible, what should be done? For all who assist, I offer these ideas.

Because the user needs a model for understanding the possible behaviors of an institution, it is important to present yourself. Tell your own stories. Refer to your own experiences and questions as a learner, especially those that linger or that seem to be more important than others. Mention what you *don't* know enough about yet, and how you would like to learn more. Let people know you are not done learning.

Because we see only the surface of an institution, it is important to refer to knowledge, its dimensions and processes, and its sources. Talk about inquiry, research, the discovery of data, the construction of knowledge. Carry a relevant book around, and sometimes wave the book around as you talk. When the moment is right, talk about the book, or the realm of study that surrounds you, and describe the possibilities of learning that wait nearby.

Because our focus is often narrow, encourage learning elsewhere. Perhaps there is a small but continuous set of questions shared across institutions. Refer people to the immense network of institutions that can compose a relevant, useful configuration of cultural education. Make the references specific and purposeful; extend the user's horizon in this way.

Talk about human beings making and thinking, because we lose sight of the handwork in things. Talk about hands and minds, handmade objects, grounded, breakthrough knowledge. Everyone needs a living model of industry or inquiry, another person we might learn from. We also need to be reminded often that human beings stand behind things: we only see their traces, and we need to know their processes and how they are still present.

Emphasize feelings and thoughts; what we come to know in a cultural institution has an effect on us. We ought to encourage users to reflect and speak about their feelings by doing these things ourselves. When a user or learner asks for data, definitions, or explanations of missing connections, we can fill in the gaps or refer to a source. Beyond this, however, I think it is more important to talk about fascination and boredom, pleasure and sadness, wonder and exhilaration, as they can be experienced in the institution. Learning (being rapt) is an experience of being seized or taken away (rapture), as by a raptor, a falcon. Our institutions, and those who hope to rescue the users in them, need to let people know that it is important to feel, and that energy comes from both caring and being carried away.

Each of us bears a record we do not easily talk about, yet we might express ourselves through it without compromising our privacy or exposing our vulnerability, if the circumstances are right. We have all felt confused and challenged. We have all felt stirrings at the edges of a great problem. To understand change and transformation in others, I believe, requires that we examine our own lives for moments of insight and possibility. Knowing the challenges we have met, we may be able to express them to others, not as teachers or advisors, but as empathic agents. When we encounter challenging complexities that slow us and perplex us (we might say to another learner), we need think ourselves forward, reflect on what we know now, and restore the possibilities of learning.

The most encouraging aspects of learning occur in moments we may barely notice. We make observations of everyday experiences, and see how day-to-day perceptions can evolve and encompass great changes over time. We experience epiphanies—moments of surprising response, breakthrough insights, and flashes or explosions of awareness. We construct surprising connections between concrete observations and abstract ideas. We revise our continuing questions, and we refine unknowns we have wondered about more than once. Something read or experienced relates the world inside the institution to the world outside the institution. At times, a museum or library can lead us to excitement and energy, at other times to entropy and chaos.

Every user, probably at all times, needs an advocate nearby: a guide, a teacher, a specialist, an agent for the learner in us.

Everyone deserves the opportunity and ability to feel that even small possibilities are worth pursuing and will make a difference in one's life. Everyone deserves to know that his or her questions are bridges. And so are memories and conversations. To think together is to build a bridge. To speak a question aloud is to build a bridge. We teach, we instruct by being able to listen and respond as well as by being able to talk, and by assisting our partners to cross the bridge we build together whenever we speak.

I have come to believe that every conversation should end with a connection, and perhaps a conscious step beyond where we had been. There are countless moments of possible connection in American cultural institutions every day, whenever a person enters and pauses, whenever a person asks a question, and whenever someone is willing to extend a lifeline and effect a needed rescue.

THE HEURISTIC

Speaking to docents at the North Carolina Museum of Art in January 2005 about rescuing the user, I suggested the need for an institutional heuristic, a way to ask consistent questions in conversation with people who stand before works of art asking about meaning. Librarians know the value of such questions, having to do with the kind of information a person needs, previous thoughts or experiences with the topic, and the kinds of connections a learner hopes to make through his or her experiences. As a reference librarian, I would approach library users with the question, "Are you finding what you need?" and then I would work from their response toward a useful discovery.

When I speak about the use of a heuristic in museums, I proceed from a similar assumption about learners: a conversation is often useful and encouraging. And I suggest that there are fundamental unknowns surrounding every museum object that can help to open its origins and character for even the most experienced user. Encouraged by the librarian, the users I encountered in the reference collection could identify their questions with help; encouraged by the educator or docent, the users of museums will similarly find grounds for observations, reflections, and inquiries of their own. By clarifying its heuristic foundations, an institution can offer its users exemplary ways of thinking about objects, and—in the words of the original 1870 mission statement of the Metropolitan Museum of Art—engage in "encouraging and developing the study of the fine arts, and the application of arts to manufacture and practical life, of advancing the general knowledge of kindred subjects, and, to that end, of furnishing popular instruction."[2]

Supplementing that original statement in 2000, the Trustees of the Metropolitan Museum affirmed those intentions and offered substantial language that applies across museums of all kinds.[3] The affirmation says that the museum will collect "works of art that are the finest and most representative of their kind from around the globe and from all periods of history, including the present," and it extends that affirmation to include the preservation, study, and exhibition of those objects. This direct, exemplary, and articulate statement goes on to express the Metropolitan's mission to "stimulate appreciation for and advance knowledge of works of art . . . at all levels" and "service of the public" across "the widest possible audience in a spirit of inclusiveness," including the intention "to increase public understanding of the Museum's goals." In these words, likely to be replicated in some form or variation across the entire museum world, I find the grounding for a museum's heuristic.

What are the guiding questions of the Metropolitan Museum? They are embedded in the mission. Why is this work the finest and most representative of its kind? In what ways might it be appreciated and understood? What are the goals of the museum in presenting this object in this way? How might these goals be served by a person observing the object here today? These are simple questions, but they ought to form the basis for every thoughtful visit to the Met. What if each docent or educator spoke those questions aloud at the beginning of each conversation with the museum's users? What if those questions, or variations on them, were published in museum guides, admission ticket stubs, or on small cards available at every service desk?

I tend to offer my students guiding questions that are at once directive and generative.[4] I offer them as questions that have value in relation to many kinds of experiences and multiple kinds of objects; I hope they are broad enough to be useful in multiple museum contexts without requiring extensive expertise or didacticism. The intention of the questions that follow—the questions I offered to docents at the North Carolina Museum of Art—was to develop a set of four approaches that might advance understanding of any artwork, artifact, or museum experience centered on a made object.

For such questions to have consequences, it would be useful for museum users to have access to a small collection of resources in print and electronic forms, or to prepare "user's handbooks" comprising diary entries, letters, critical comments, or biographical statements about the creators of specific works, or the cultural systems or faith perspectives of which they are a part. Access to information always empowers the user. When objects are placed in galleries, their sensual interest and contextual power are reduced by the setting and its expectations, and by the presence of other strong experiences nearby. In part, it is my intention to use questions, access to information, and individual observations to restore the potential for an object to seize its observer as a fresh experience.

When we talk about a work of skill and inspiration, we ought to talk about the artist's human impulse to make something original and fresh, an object or a combination of images that the world has not yet seen. The imitative and banal are by definition outside our interests. We should begin these conversations about art with the assumption that the maker of a work was led by an urgency to make the world and the self more complete or more whole by making something new.

If we make this assumption, our questions in museums might change. We might become less interested in history as a grand sweep across a century's featureless landscape and more interested in art works and art makers situated within a place, a culture, and a time. The legacies of artists and artisans are not accidental; what they have left behind to be gathered by curators and scholars is meant to have survived as a record or an example, or as an expression of human need that could take no other form. Our naïve questions may also draw us to consider the roles of artworks and their makers in our own time, and what, when given to us by the hands of our contemporaries, remains incomplete for us.

Every museum, even every library, might usefully construct and clarify its own heuristic, a set of questions that places a collection in the lives of its users by expressing its central values, the questions it strives to answer as it acquires new objects, and the possible themes that move throughout the setting. Many years ago, at the American Museum of Natural History, it occurred to me that a brief heuristic about the nature of evolution would serve me well in every gallery, including those galleries devoted to human adaptations and cultures.

For a wonderful year, I would use that museum each week, and as I did the great structure of evidence and thought would lead naturally to my questions. What do I see now? What do I see next? What stories or continuities might connect them? What part of my previous experience or imagination informs these connections? It does not matter where one stands, in the museum of art or history or natural sciences; human change and cultural complexity seem appropriate ideas to stand at the center of any heuristic: the conditions of a complex setting and population, reactions to threat and risk, attempts to establish continuities and order, challenges from environments outside the organism's control.

Thinking critically about a complex organism in response to its environment also extended beyond that great museum, and could be applied in Central Park across the street, or at the New-York Historical Society on an adjacent corner, with slight adaptations. For me, the heuristic of twenty years ago still works, and still has value in a setting where any organism—amoeba, mastodon, monarch and viceroy, Inuit, scientist, anthropologist, astronaut, sculptor—adapts in order to live.

Cultural institutions cannot deny the heuristics actively engaged in shaping their collections, or in fulfilling their desire for "service of the public." These values operate steadily in decisions made at all levels of institutional planning and design. Why has a curator or bibliographer interpreted or developed the collection in this way? How do collections of artifacts or information relate to life in the world outside this place? How do the planners of a new museum or library think of its content and presentation as a response to a series of questions its everyday users might ask?

What small number of questions will capture the purpose of the collection and assist its users to understand how to think constructively within it? Under what conditions are such questions intended to be answerable? No question will be a perfect mechanism, nor will the response it elicits always be articulate and direct. When a museum intentionally reduces its didacticism in favor of a conversation, it has understood that a cultural institution is not a test. Answers—or better, informed and thoughtful responses—might not be possible at the moment a question is asked, though informed professionals, educators, and docents should be able to contribute what they know gently to the process.

The purposes of heuristic questions in the museum are not to elicit facts or other data, but to clarify the original contexts of works and their makers and authors. They also can serve as models for the subsequent questions a museum or library user will ask without the presence of an informed guide; this is why those guides, educators, curators, and museum directors need to express their own unanswered questions in public as well.

FOUR PUBLIC QUESTIONS

The intention of my first question is to remind the learner (and the institution) that the hand and mind of a human being were responsible for the making of the work before us. This concept of making implies a human imagination as well, and human constraints.

> What has been brought here? Who made this object?
> *There is an identity, situation, and role for the maker or artist in a culture.*
> *It is a formative part of every work. How can we see it in the object?*

These questions are intended to encourage speculation and inquiry about the situated human being who made the work. It may also encourage the learner to contemplate the skills and cognitive processes of making the item, its author as a learner, and the potentially obscure motives that brought the work into the world. The work itself may represent a problem its maker has had to solve, or a process of art where the maker finds an identity and purpose. *A person made this. What does this mean?*

The somewhat flat questions of the heuristic can yield clusters of ancillary questions about the making of the object. What can we know about the person who made this object? Under what circumstances was it made? What tools and processes were necessary in the making of this object? What challenges are apparent in the evidence of this work? What mastery was needed to overcome these challenges? Why would the maker make this?

I hope to suggest a series of perspectives or angles that allow a museum user to express a response through questions. The second question assumes that some strengths of a work are discernible in the piece itself; these can be understood as its effect on the person who sees it. By asking a question, the strength or subtlety of the object can be considered and discussed.

> How does the work have meaning and power?
> *An object implies and communicates intentions, impulses,*
> *constraints, and possibilities.*
> *What evidence do we sense in the work of the maker's guiding intentions?*

Aspects of a work can break through to the observer, almost rolling off the material itself. What would this breaking through be called in the art museum? Knowledge? Information? Passion? Experiment? Discovery? Sensation? Privacy? Isolation? Self-presentation? Influence? Naïveté? Joy? Artlessness? Patronage? Politics? War? Conquest? Dissent? Economics? Environment? Industry? Poverty? Privilege? Commodity? Scarcity? Aspiration? Culture? Tribe? Society? Rite? Awe? Fear? Devotion? Worship? Sexuality? Mourning? Anger? Narrative?

The third question I offer here responds to the need for the museum to make its values and purposes more transparent to the user by describing elements of the thinking applied to collections and their curation.

Why has it been collected by the museum?
An object has its own purpose in a collection of objects.
In some way, each object collected redefines or
confirms the meaning of the collection.

The question is direct: it asks why a particular work has been collected. The subsequent questions below offer forms of explanation, to allow the collector's thinking to become more public, part of the museum user's deepening attention to the object and what a *collection* of objects implies.

How does the work help to fulfill the mission of the museum? Does the object capture or demonstrate mastery? What do other artists say about it? Is the object an exemplar? Does it capture themes or ideas that characterize a particular genius or influence? Can we compare it usefully to other works in the collection, or widely known works held elsewhere? Does the work exemplify the values of a culture? Does this work fulfill an aspect of the collection plan? Does the work demonstrate a theme that has special value to the collection? Does the work add to our collection of works by an individual, or a group of individuals? Does the work show a strong and illuminating relationship to other objects in the collection?

The question reminds us of the collection as a whole construction, a conscious attempt to be comprehensive or selective in particular ways. It also implies the many ways that an artwork has meaning, how it relates to other works, and how the museum has sought to express its purpose by collecting it.

The final question I suggest for the heuristic helps the user to understand that no question is ever likely to end and that all questions are likely to stimulate others. When we assume that we have asked questions well, and considered the objects before us, we can also pause to think about the unending aspects of artworks and museum experiences. The museum that acknowledges this has developed a purposeful way to invite users to return to the museum for subsequent experiences, for special programs, and to reconsider the collection in the future. Moreover, when unanswered questions are brought to the foreground, logical transitions can be made among cultural institutions, public libraries, other museums, and the cultural resources of the Web.

What do our best questions leave unanswered?
However well we think, unknowns remain.
These are always welcome in the museum and the library.

In a cultural institution, nothing is begun and nothing is taken away without a good question. Nothing is changed, nothing is provoked, art does not affect us, cultures do not grow, and people do not become stronger without a question that leads them forward. I will adapt my guiding questions continuously to make them more functional and more illuminating as I try them out in different places, on different examples and evidence. This is merely one learner's mindful way to observe and experience in cultural institutions, and eventually to think critically in the situations of our lives where our learning and our rescue can happen.

What makes good questions happen? What makes them evolve and change? What might the change mean? If the object holds a story, who tells that story? How do we recognize objects that hold the evidences of our selves?

NOTES

1. In the *New York Times Magazine* on September 22, 2002, an interview with Garry Kasparov, the chess grandmaster, addressed his upcoming match with a computer, not unlike the match he played against IBM's Deep Blue computer in 1997, an event described in the news as the brain's last stand against the machine. (Kasparov lost, and somehow the world did not disappear into dust.)

Q. What's at stake in this match?
A. It's not the final battle—the human brain's "last stand," as *Newsweek* put it five years ago. I treat it more like a continuation of a very important scientific experiment. Where else can we compete with computers? Either humans will be stronger in creativity, or computers will win with the brute force of calculation. The brute force of calculation on one side, and humans' creativity on the other side.
Q. You've said that while computers will be stronger than humans, humans will always create the art in chess.
A. You know, it will not be just who is going to win the match. It will be whether we can win one single game. I'm quite serious. The experiment goes on as long as we are winning one single game. If we can win one came, we're in business. For a while we'll be able to win the match. I think I'm still the favorite. But I'm not sure it will last. But one game? I think we can win one game for quite a while. [William Ferguson, "Check This," *New York Times Magazine*, 22 Sept. 2002, 19.]

2. Charter of The Metropolitan Museum of Art, State of New York, Laws of 1870, Chapter 197, passed April 13, 1870 and amended L. 1898, ch. 34; L. 1908, ch. 219.

3. The Metropolitan Museum of Art, "Mission Statement," <http://www.metmuseum.org/annual_report/2003_2004/pdf/o4-mission-statement.pdf> (18 November 2005).

4. When I take students to the North Carolina Museum of History and the North Carolina Museum of Natural Sciences in Raleigh, I distribute these questions

to guide the day's observations: What has been brought here and how has it been organized? How do you imagine an original context for this object or specimen? What information would be useful to fully understand its origin, function, and situation? How did it evolve? Of what is it made? Was it made by a human being? How do you know? Have you ever seen something like this before? Where? When? In how many ways might this object be categorized? What other items or specimens of its kind might have surrounded it in its original world? Of what systems or processes was it once a part? What everyday, familiar phenomena or experiences are evoked by this example? What is the intention of those who collected and brought it here? What is the design or plan of the collection and its presentation? For you, what is the key question to ask—the central unknown—in this collection? What does the collection encourage you to think about? How do your best, most provocative questions happen here? How do your questions change? What is going on here?

6

READING BEYOND THE MUSEUM

The resonant exhibition inspires and extends the capable mind; original experiences of depth and power make us want to know more. The capacious mind, once engaged, cannot easily turn away. When we use a museum well, our mind is given over, opened up, to the museum, if only for the time it takes for us to see the collected evidence. If that powerful, resonant moment might extend beyond the museum in ways that are easy to inspire—ways of reading—the great museum could become the instrument for learning it has too rarely been.

When it is successful, reading in museums does not simply *tell* us about the world that stands beyond the museum; reading is in itself a surrogate experience of the world, a process of thought, interaction, and relationship that implicates us first into the captive life of the object before us, and then into the larger world where it began. By reading a generative label or wall text, the museum user is compelled to consider the logic and wholeness of something that cannot be present, but is represented by something that is perpetually present in the object or the specimen. The fossil frond invokes the lost fern, still alive in the Cenozoic era.

In any museum, a reading that implies the reality of a voice, a story, or an original context has cognitive consequences. Wolfgang Iser, theoretician of what happens in readers' minds, writes, "As the reader passes through the various perspectives offered by the text, and relates the different views and patterns to one another, he sets the work in motion, and so sets himself in motion, too."[1] Reading sends the mind elsewhere, beyond what is here.

This essay considers reading as an opportunity to sustain the extended themes and values of the museum beyond the experience of the museum itself. The museum provides models, templates, or frames for understanding and reading the worldly systems beyond it. Its stories, patterns, and continuities

57

provide the basis for seeing and reading our own interior experiences and insights, as we interpret them in relationship to larger narratives. And reading itself—actual engagements with texts on walls and in hands, and conversations among other readers about those engagements—holds the potential for deepening the gifts of energy, attention, and presence brought into the museum by its users.

Reading always—*always*—cultivates human intelligence, a goal described as John Dewey's "overriding interest" by Maxine Greene, who writes that Dewey's intention was "that persons would become reflective, deliberative, 'mindful' with respect to their own lived (and shared) situations."[2] This is an interest museums and their educators share. The museum might also take to heart Greene's own recognition that "literacy in a pluralist society depends to a considerable degree on the capacity to interpret, to identify with other points of view, as well as to explain." Museums express pluralism, explain the other, and interpret the different; these are stimulating forms of literacy for reading the world as it is and might become. Greene writes, "We need to invent a democratic literacy, literacy for what is not yet."[3] Museums ought to participate as critical instruments in this invention of a worldly literacy beyond the moment.

READING BEYOND SALGADO

At the Ackland Art Museum on the University of North Carolina campus in Chapel Hill and at the Center for Documentary Studies at Duke University in Durham, thousands of museum users in early 2004 saw an extensive exhibition of photographs, "Migrations: Humanity in Transition," comprising scores of images made of migrants and children by the great master of social photography, Sebastião Salgado. Those museum users repeated a familiar process: they went to the museum and had a deliberate experience of gathered evidence, arranged on walls and introduced in this way:

> In 1993, Sebastião Salgado began a photographic investigation into the phenomenon of mass migration at the end of the twentieth century. For six years and in more than forty countries, he focused his lens on the plight of the dispossessed, both on the road and in the refugee camps and urban slums where they lived. According to Salgado, the migrants allowed themselves to be photographed in these conditions because they wanted their struggle to be recorded and made known.[4]

Like most exhibitions, "Migrations" presented a particular perspective on the world through artifacts. Its planners provided texts on walls and in captions, defining images and the circumstances of their making. Themes, so evident in the advertising quotation—"mass migration," "the plight of the dispossessed," "refugee camps and urban slums"—pervaded these images, made in Ecuador, India, Albania, Tanzania, and other places where war, economics, exploitation, and politics have altered forever the traditional lives of common people. While the evidence and its themes are sharply visible, the possible ways of reading the perspective on the world presented by the exhibition are not. What did users see? What unknowns were evoked? Our minds filled with images, what are we to *do*? One response is that we are obligated to read.

I asked more than thirty of my advanced students—all studying reference librarianship in the humanities and social sciences—to attend this exhibition and to provide three bibliographic citations of likely interest to an adult learner. I asked them to "imagine a serious, thoughtful inquirer—perhaps someone you know—who wishes to go beyond the exhibition and learn more." Students could suggest articles, books, encyclopedias, statistics, or any other item that bore relevance to the ideas implicit in the photographs. Among all the information they could command, their choices had no limits among history, politics, religion, migration, family, population, narrative, photography, or other arts. The suggestions were surprisingly individual and unpredictably different: of the nearly one hundred citations I received, only a handful were duplicative.[5] Each citation was a different way of reading beyond the Salgado exhibition, based on nuance and interpretation, experiences and interests. How many other ways might there be to read beyond this world of Salgado? How might reading help to construct and sustain the thinking that any great and powerful exhibition begins?

READING IS EXPLORATION

What is omnipresent is imperceptible. Nothing is more commonplace than the reading experience, and yet nothing is more unknown. Reading is such a matter of course that, at first glance, it seems there is nothing to say about it.[6]

So it seems, at first, there is nothing to say, and yet the deep literature devoted to reading is rich and generative. Louise Rosenblatt's descriptions of reading transactions—a classic approach to the teaching of literature—can be applied directly to museum experiences. Person and text, she says, are not separate entities, or antagonists daring each other to make something meaningful; rather, in the moment of the reading event, the reader and text engage to construct each other mutually, in a "to-and-fro" transaction.[7] Reading in the museum, we similarly engage in a collaborative process with evidence and words, and (because we are not blank slates) we remember the world beyond the museum, and ourselves in that world as well. Our ability to do this, Rosenblatt says, is a reflection of "the multiple nature of the human being, [the human] potentialities for many more selves and kinds of experience than any one being could express."[8] We might say of the museum user, as Rosenblatt says of her subject, "An intense response to a work will have its roots in capacities and experiences already present in the personality and mind of the reader."[9]

Reading is one way to explore the private world within, and the empirical world beyond ourselves. As we read and experience, we imagine a situation based on evidence. We see the circumstances of history or environment, or the intentions of an artist in our own deeply personal images; we may see ourselves as actors in the landscape as well.

However far our minds can imagine and however well words can describe a place elsewhere (while our bodies stay here), we experience, occupy, and live through another reality. It is not a merely literary idea to say, as Ralph Ellison did, that "What one reads becomes part of what one sees and feels."[10] To read is to come into a mind of our own through the guiding questions and observations of other minds; it is to negotiate the possibilities of the world we may be unable to see for ourselves.

Our reading of texts, labels, and objects takes us beyond the museum when we recognize patterns in the environment, or when a museum experience evokes the deeply hidden dimensions of emotion that tacitly configure our insights and recognitions. Every invisible part of us—tacit knowing, memory, language, aspiration—becomes involved in the reading event. To borrow words from Rosenblatt, our reading is "a *living through*, not simply *knowledge about.*"[11]

Reading, our omnipresent yet imperceptible cognitive work, is a way of constructing ourselves. In Dewey, Vygotsky, and Bruner[12] we find agreement on the ways that language builds concepts, synthesizes continuities, and constructs coherent, meaningful stories. Naming objects and concepts allows relationships among them; we can reconfigure patterns and think more complex thoughts. Bruner's work leads to Wolfgang Iser, who describes the reader as being drawn into a text by "completing" or "performing" it, interpreting implications, filling in gaps, in such a way that the reader's experience does not arise from the printed word, so much as from "the interaction between text and reader."[13] The reader sorts out the implied connection from the explicit narrative, or finds a truth within the fine print, where one brief insight might reorganize everything we had thought. In its most constructive ways, reading is the completion of a text, the filling-in of blanks by the reader. Iser calls this "the play of the text."[14] Such play—in the sense of having flexibility and litheness—engages thinking and the exploration of possibilities.

There is a certain purpose to advocacy for reading in museums. Most simply, reading is seeking, reading is thinking. To read is to encounter evidence and to construe contexts; reading allows the user to surround an object, to interpret its original place, or to infer its original emergence, otherwise not in evidence. Reading in the museum is a transaction among the mindful user, the sensory details of experience, and the construction of implications. In these implications, the most generative consequences are founded. Against surrounding experiences of discontinuity, reading is a form of energy to counter simplification, reduction, and fragmentation. Reading introduces connections and complexities, constructs questions, and leads the user forward. In our relations with texts, we experience through reading what we might initially think of as a mere thread, when in fact it is a form of intellect and connection, a way toward becoming.

A READING OF THE WORLD

We need ways to work with our intelligence when we are among collections, ways to construct the possible voices silent in mute objects. Discussing the artifactual nature of both museum and book collections, G. Thomas Tanselle cites Anna Somers Cocks, a curator at the Victoria and Albert Museum, who "spoke of puzzling over artifacts 'until their language became clear.'" Tanselle goes on, "All artifacts can be read, once their language is learned, for what they have to tell about their own production and about the place they held in the lives of those who previously possessed them. All are evidences of human activity, manifestations of the physical basis of culture."[15] It is not pure metaphor to speak of reading the visual characteristics of physical objects; we experience them in much the same way as we read maps: observing details and contours, indicators of context and location, and the signatures of change, process, and place. As learners, we look for signs. Tanselle writes, "The world itself is a museum, of course. . . . We cannot avoid reading artifacts as signatures of intellect: they are an inescapable part of our physical surroundings."[16] He reminds us that Joyce put Stephen Daedalus in place to read "the signatures of all things." For any reader of contemporary poetry, this brings to mind William Carlos Williams, who wrote in the early pages of his great work *Paterson*, "Say it! No ideas but in things."[17] We might carve those words above museum doorways.

In my experience, the transformative value of a museum lies in its construction of knowledge, the ordering of evidence at hand in ways that respect my capacity to think and read for myself. Taxonomy, geography, genetics, time—or any other system that makes the lived world coherent—can be interpreted as a way of framing the information given. When a constructed frame is rich, explicit, and detailed—like the planetarium view of the starry night sky—a user can transfer the image, nearly intact, to the world outside. When the frame includes alternative views, questions, and interpretations, or suggests a way to go forward as a learner, the museum stimulates new ideas and intentions for action in the world. The inspired user buys a star atlas and good binoculars, and begins to read the sky.

A constructive template, like the model of the sky on a planetarium ceiling, is the first of several ways for the museum to provide an organizing architecture for reading and interpreting in the world. The frame given by the museum will inevitably be incomplete, but this is a good thing in any purposeful education. The user's transactions—like the reader's—are required to advance and fulfill the unfinished structure, perhaps carried within the learner as a series of questions. In several ways, a museum can offer explicit frames for reading the world beyond its walls.

The museum transmits frameworks of knowledge and value. When a collection of objects is presented in the museum, it can communicate a structure that has probative value or heuristic value in itself. The museum shows us patterns in art works, or generations of technology and innovation, or simply in the empirical methods used to replicate and confirm the knowledge on display. These are definitive ways of constructing the world, and we may carry their implied perspectives beyond the museum, for use elsewhere. Such frameworks are probably distinct from museum to museum; no two institutions think, collect, label, or describe identically; every invented structure has an imprint, a design, and an epistemology it transmits tacitly to the user. To grasp this frame is to read deeply beyond the collection, toward reorganizing our own image of the world.

The museum presents a lens. The lens may be literal, a form of optical instrument: a microscope, a telescope, a simple magnifier, or a corrective screen to provide focus. Literally, this lens clarifies and brings visual evidence closer to our eyes and minds. Or the lens is metaphoric, perhaps methodological: Here is how the museum sees the objects it collects, how it senses the tensions among them, how it envisions their contexts. Here is how the museum interprets the artifact in a particular tradition, as a specific kind of evidence. How does the curator see this object, or this evidence? This is how the museum also wants you to see it. To see through the museum's lens is to learn a way of viewing the world apart from the museum itself.

The museum implies the whole fabric in the small sample. Thirty Iroquois masks exemplify all Iroquois masks. "View of Delft" shows us the particular world of Vermeer's experience. Diplodocus is an emblem of the Jurassic era. The kitchen of 1955 captures whole a domestic context of the time. The living history farm is how it was to plant and labor and learn to read the sky. The first telephone or motion picture camera, the Spirit of St. Louis, the Volkswagen camper, a pair of ruby red slippers, twisted rubble from New York: all of these are more than what they appear to be. Because we cannot ever retrieve the whole reality, the museum provides a piece of it for our conjectures. The small artifact, or juxtaposed groups of artifacts, can open a much larger and more challenging narrative than the immediate context implies.[18] In the moment of observation, our task is to weave the immediate sensory experience into a pattern that clarifies a larger and more challenging story. Later the experience is extended by reflection beyond it.

The museum is a place of further implication. Our regard for the object implies that there is value in knowing its origin and purpose; the presence of the object in a collection implies an integrity and character of its own, among other pieces. Nowhere is this more evident than among collections of faith objects, for example, where even a modest image can imply solace and inspiration, and project a relationship with the infinite. A faith object implies practices and beliefs, rites and duties. It is part of a system of texts and guiding ideas. Faith objects imply an image of the sacred; devotion to these objects implies a motive of hope and transcendence. Relationships and communions of faith are conducted through such objects, often simply by gazing at them. When we look across different objects of faith traditions, we can sense a resonance among the spiritual experiences and traditions they represent, and the possibilities of sacred truth they imply. Faith objects allow us to grasp the dimensions of an essentially private invisible world.

The museum assists us to read the formative story. If we are learners, we look for an existing vocabulary of human structures, motives, and values, in order to speak of them. We turn again and again to the large stories that shape our approach to the unknown. Darwin tells the formative story of evolution; Edison tells us the formative story of practical insight. Basic, fundamental stories help us to understand change and adaptation. Empirical methods allow us to understand certain kinds of problem solving. Tensions between immovable forces and ensuing conflicts are formative stories applicable to warfare and industry. These are formative because their familiar ideas can shape our own concepts of continuity and process. They give us a way to start thinking of something we do not yet understand.

I will never penetrate the canvases of Cy Twombly, nor will I ever tire of trying, but when I think about the formative images of cave markings or graffiti as I recollect his work, I begin to understand something (I think). I can never see enough of the star clusters in Cygnus in summer, though each time look up I find myself dizzy from the starlight. When I envision myself in an entirely dark world on the Great Plains a century ago, I see the patterns more clearly. Nor will I ever grasp in depth the heart of the Qur'án, the Talmud, or the Book of Job, but one reads on, just as one looks on, to see what is possible to know and believe.

The formative stories to be told in museums are endless. The geologic story is formative. War is a formative story. Tribal relationships and explanations compose a formative story. The trickster is a formative story. Ceremonies, ritual practices, and chants are formative stories; when we understand them we have read part of a larger human pattern.

READING SUSTAINS THOUGHT

Every museum has thoughtful users who strive to understand what they have not yet understood. This too is a formative human story, the one that drives the user in the museum. However variable, every museum is a vessel filled with information; and yet, in my experience, museum spaces are typically void of visible books, recommended readings, or bibliographic citations. One important way to take up an advocacy for reading is the simplest: provide examples of readings that illuminate the museum and its contents. (The Denver Art Museum does this brilliantly, in spaces set apart for users to pause and read. Reynolda House, a fine small American Art museum in Winston-Salem, North Carolina, casually leaves copies of books—Whitman, Fitzgerald, Emily Dickinson—on furniture near paintings, merely suggesting the links between the visual and literary.) Exhibition bibliographies might easily appear in brochures, on bookmarks and Web sites, and in museum shops. This is the most direct way for the museum to cause something to happen as a result of its exhibitions.

It is costly to produce grand catalogs, but many inexpensive, existing books can be adopted as guides to an exhibition. With local adaptations and supplements, standard handbooks of art, flora and fauna, American history, natural sciences, astronomy, and cultural artifacts can be endorsed for gallery use. A small set of chosen, guiding works could become an ancillary toolkit for the self-directed learner in the museum. The extraordinary popularity of reading groups in libraries, workplaces, and communities might inspire similar conversations among museum members and local museum users. Potential reading choices are vast.[19] Stories themselves are virtually endless; the value of storytelling, public readings, film discussions, and forums on issues is immeasurable. Museums cannot do enough of this; the wider the presentation of demonstrably relevant concepts and ideas in the museum, the greater the value of the museum to its supporters, communities, and staff members.

Museums should use current newspapers, magazines, and research articles, where appropriate, to confirm the continuities between museum evidence and everyday issues. Every day we find fresh reporting about health, history, the environment, science, and the arts. The front page of my newspaper this morning described the loss of more than one million forest acres in my state during the past twelve years.[20] What does this mean to the mission of our natural history museum? The front page of this morning's *New York Times* carries an article about Coney Island Avenue in Brooklyn, where Turks, Hasidim and other Orthodox Jews, Saudis, assorted Muslims, Cubans, Pakistanis, Haitians, Russians, and others from former Soviet nations, live, eat, work, and talk.[21] There are human stories here. What great or small New York museum might tell them, and help all its citizens to read the new, evolving world of Coney Island Avenue?

Museums and libraries exist everywhere in places of diversity and opportunity. What does the museum hold that can invite, inspire, and inform? How does the public library offer itself to its users? What might the museum learn from the public library? How might a museum user read the newspaper differently after a thoughtful museum experience of Islamic culture, African belief systems, Holocaust narratives, or forced migrations brought on by war and politics? Why do we rarely hear relevant curatorial comments on current events in the museum? How can the lessons of contemporary experience be related to museum collections? How does a curator, or a museum educator, read a newspaper?

READING, A MUSEUM VALUE

I believe that the museum should remind us in every way that the contents of the museum are not complete, that the environment still evolves, that art continues to be made, and that history is never in the past. For educative museums, there are lessons to be learned, and experiments to be undertaken, if we are to understand the nature of reading, and how it is a process of transformation, as well as an essential instrumentality for living in the world. Every person's literacy needs to grow.

Begin with the certainty that new acts of language—new words, new combinations, and new descriptions of knowledge and feeling—are essential parts of museum learning. Whatever our new knowledge in the museum, it is critical for us to say it aloud, to write or express it in silence to ourselves, as it emerges. Otherwise it will be uncaptured and lost. It is not difficult to consider the possibilities of the museum experience as a bridge to new languages and new conversations. Literacy learning in museums would hold the promise of vivid examples, international artifacts, and dedicated conversations between a learner and a tutor. The museum is a perfect venue for learning to express halting words in a safe, nondidactic environment.

We have information to advocate and communities to touch. Museums must be learning and reaching toward other institutions if they are to experience the fullness of their communities. We have especially important alliances to form around reading. Public libraries are essential to embrace; they have lessons about independent learning and public conversations to teach museums. Most museums already are connected to schools and other academic institutions, but the advocacy of reading is a natural link between classroom processes and museum inquiries. There are largely unexplored community links to consider: shelters, hospitals, adult residencies, and prisons. The museum's themes and experiences can illuminate such places. Museum outreach involving readings, observations, and conversations can extend the museum into places where learning, recovery, and reflection might save or extend or renew lives.

Nothing has changed in the world so dramatically in recent years as our relationship to words, languages, and stories. Information flows without end. And yet, at times, nothing has remained so steadfastly the same: we read, and the narrative entrances us. We turn to tell others what has happened to us; we cannot wait to communicate the newest thing we know. Among thoughtful and engaged people, the leading edge of our lives is also the reading edge; and so it should be in museums.

NOTES

1. Wolfgang Iser, "Interaction between Text and Reader," in *The Reader in the Text: Essays on Audience and Interpretation*, ed. Susan R. Suleiman and Inge Crosman (Princeton: Princeton University Press, 1980), 106.

2. Maxine Greene, "Philosophy, Reason, and Literacy," *Review of Educational Research* 54 (Winter 1984): 551.

3. Greene, "Philosophy," 556, 558.

4. [Exhibition advertisement], "Migrations: Humanity in Transition," February 1–March 28, 2004, Ackland Art Museum (Chapel Hill, NC) and Center for Documentary Studies (Durham, NC).

5. Here are several exemplary titles and authors among student recommendations: *Encyclopedia of Genocide* (Israel W. Charny); *Imagine Coexistence: Restoring Humanity After Violent Ethnic Conflict* (Antonia Chayes and Martha L. Minow); *Children and Play in the Holocaust* (George Eisen); *We Wish to Inform You That Tomorrow We Will Be Killed with Our Families* (Philip Gourevitch); *The Impact of War on Children* (Machel Graça); *The Limits of Humanitarian Intervention: Genocide in Rwanda* (Alan J. Kuperman); *Witness in Our Time: Working Lives of Documentary Photographers* (Ken Light); *The Suitcase: Refugee Voices from Bosnia and Croatia* (Julie Mertus, et al.); *Regarding the Pain of Others* (Susan Sontag).

6. Tzvetan Todorov, "Reading as Conversation," in *The Reader in the Text: Essays on Audience and Interpretation*, ed. Susan R. Suleiman and Inge Crosman (Princeton: Princeton University Press, 1980), 67.

7. Louise M. Rosenblatt, *Literature as Exploration*, 5th ed. (New York: Modern Language Association, 1995), 292.

8. Rosenblatt, *Literature*, 40.

9. Rosenblatt, *Literature*, 41.

10. Ralph Ellison, quoted in J. Kevin Graffagnino, *Only in Books: Writers, Readers, & Bibliophiles on Their Passion* (Madison, WI: Madison House, 1996), 77.

11. Rosenblatt, *Literature*, 38.

12. See, for example, the discussion of Vygotsky in Jerome Bruner, *Actual Minds, Possible Worlds* (Cambridge, MA: Harvard University Press, 1986), 74–76. Also see Jerome Bruner, *Making Stories: Law, Literature, Life* (Cambridge, MA: Harvard University Press, 2002), 3–35, 89–107, passim.

13. Iser, "Interaction," 111.

14. Wolfgang Iser, *Prospecting: From Reader Response to Literary Anthropology* (Baltimore: Johns Hopkins University Press, 1989), 249–261.

15. G. Thomas Tanselle, "Libraries, Museums, and Reading," *Raritan* 12 (Summer 1992): 66–67.

16. Tanselle, "Libraries," 81

17. William Carlos Williams, *Paterson* (New York: New Directions, 1963), 18.

18. For example, consider the world conjured up by a Klan hood gently placed in a baby carriage. See Fred Wilson, *Mining the Museum* (New York, NY: New Press, 1994).

19. Here are several examples, with varied relevance among museums; but all are likely to stimulate conversations and insights, wherever they are read and discussed: Mihaly Csikszentmihalyi, *The Evolving Self: A Psychology for the Third Millennium* (New York: HarperCollins, 1993); Ellen Dissanayake, *What is Art For?* (Seattle, WA: University of Washington Press, 1988); Paul John Eakin, *How Our Lives Become Stories:*

Making Selves (Ithaca, NY: Cornell University Press, 1999); Howard Gardner, *The Disciplined Mind: Beyond Facts and Standardized Tests, the K–12 Education that Every Child Deserves* (New York: Penguin Books, 2000); Bill McKibben, *Enough: Staying Human in an Engineered Age* (New York: Henry Holt and Company, 2003).

20. Wade Rawlins, "N.C. Forests Falling Fast," *The News & Observer* (Raleigh, NC), 26 March 2004, 1A.

21. Andy Newman, "On Brooklyn's Avenue of Babel, Cultures Entwine," *The New York Times* [National Edition], 26 March 2004, A1.

7

FIVE THOUGHTFUL EXERCISES

The Five Faiths Project, an ongoing initiative funded by the Henry Luce Foundation, brought religion scholars, practitioners of five spiritual traditions, and museum educators to the Ackland Art Museum at the University of North Carolina at Chapel Hill for the first of three colloquies addressing museum objects from various religious heritages.[1] The premise of the gathering was that museum collections contain objects central to spiritual practices, and these can be used to create conversations among museum visitors, inviting exploration of the often private and privileged assumptions that informed the making of these objects. During these gatherings, the Ackland exhibited faith objects and images from its collections. Enlisting these artifacts from vastly different traditions and beliefs, the colloquists discussed the problems of portraying the subtleties of spiritual practices to audiences who may not share their premises.

The objects that served in our conversations—paintings, sculptures, vessels, icons, ritual implements, illuminated texts, and so on—were broadly distributed among Christian, Buddhist, Muslim, Hindu, and Judaic traditions. The museum curators and educators developed galleries and labels guided by the assumption that sacred artifacts and images embody messages that allow faith practices to become clarified and comparable when contemplated in the secular space of the museum.

One value of the project was to bring all five traditions to the table equally, using the instrumentality of aesthetic representations to facilitate communication among them. On its Web site, the museum describes the purpose of the project in the following way:

> The Five Faiths Project introduces, with original works of art from the Ackland's multicultural permanent collection, the beliefs and practices of

Buddhism, Christianity, Hinduism, Islam and Judaism—religious traditions that have a strong presence in North Carolina and generally in American society today. It is with the idea of assisting communication between these new faith communities and the established Protestant community that the project came into being. The Five Faiths Project is founded on the conviction that centering conversations about faith traditions on works of art originally used in worship promotes objective and thoughtful consideration of those traditions, while also inhibiting unproductive ideological debates that impede tolerant understanding and learning.[2]

A group of approximately twenty-five colloquists participated in the three gatherings. The attendees comprised (in the words of the museum): "museum professionals, scholars of religion, local and national religious leaders and contemporary artists . . . invited to consider and discuss the obstacles to and the benefits of using works of art as vehicles for teaching about world religions." A core of approximately twenty participants attended all three colloquies. During the colloquy sessions, conversations were stimulated by a series of talks and explications, using different objects and presenting the observations of different faith perspectives.

Given the composition of the gathering, the exercises described below required participants to work across religious traditions and perspectives, in part because people were led to different objects by each others' interests and expertise. Educators who engaged in this process reported having stimulating conversations, constructed around objects that (in the everyday life of museums) tend to be respected and studied but not interpreted.

The participants in the Five Faiths Colloquy were engaged in a discussion of both the promise and the problems associated with articulating values across religious traditions, using museum objects that are strongly symbolic and instrumental in religious practices. We worked under the assumption that, in American society, despite the secular nature of government and public service, an awareness of religion in everyday experience is often inescapable, and the invocation of traditional values often implies the presence of diverse and quite separate forms of worship and observance. Devoted members of faith communities do not lose their beliefs when acting in secular environments, and so it is easy to see cultural discourse permeated by individual participants' grounding in personal faiths and silent beliefs. These assumptions must also be regarded in the shadow of the events of September 11, 2001, when politics and religion fused in the most extreme manner.

If we are able to regard museums and other cultural institutions as problem-solving structures—places where thoughtful users go, anticipating that they will discover new objects, ideas, and resources to assist the cognitive, emotional, and ethical processes of living their lives—we can come to see how a secular museum space can assist people to understand religious patterns and values, and to see faith practices in a different frame from that given by media, where education is not always the leading intention. Advocates for an educative museum will grasp the possibility that, without compromising the objects held there, an emphasis on communication and explanation will help curious people to address the unfinished issues that configure cognitive experiences. As a museum observer, I am engaged by the processes and objects that inspire our wonder, the unknowns that seem to be our own continuous mysteries, and the questions that seem merely to evolve in detail and complexity no matter how much we pursue them.

Problems of religion and its expression offer fine examples of the guiding questions that never appear to be resolved—yet we love the questions no less, for all their fragmentation and elusive grace. We must learn to love our questions, and even cultivate them, because they never go away. They are artifacts we have made; they are ours. Using our questions to guide us, we craft the truths that allow continuities and insights into our changing private worlds.

When we regard the faith object as something that may assist us toward insight and renewal, we are observing a product of the human mind and hand, one that reflects a divine image emergent in the hand's work. We can assume that the faith object mediates a direct experience of devotion, and this authenticity provides us with a kind of critical evidence that can be examined with care. It holds an intimacy we rarely find in other contemplations of even the grandest secular artifacts, perhaps because it is possible to see the faith object itself as an answer to a problem, or as a link to its guiding values.

Though the faith object is a material artifact like other objects, we accept it also as a vessel or a host for the sacred voice or divine value, something given to us as evidence of remarkable excellence and grace. As scholars and practitioners made clear during our Five Faiths conversations, in the presence of the great faith object, we see and feel its power to summon a response, to evoke a divine name or theme, and to allow us to pause in awe at the evidence before us. Whether we stand inside or outside a system of beliefs, we want to know what people who are believers experience in the presence of the object. We hope to grasp its logics and central constructs. We want to know or feel its mystery or inspiration in ways that illuminate the beliefs themselves—how the faith object brings to those who respond to it some form of reconciliation, solace, contemplation, challenge, or hope.

And, because it is the way we learn, we want to go beyond the object to the critical point in our observations when we are able to tie it to something we have seen or understood in our memories or hearts. In even a small increment of this process—this going beyond the object to our own clear place of insight—we experience a change in our problem, a step toward a new form of anticipation and possible understanding. Such experiences are full of promise. The late John W. Gardner, author of *Excellence* and *No Easy Victories*, described this as self-renewal, the fundamental characteristic of being human.

How do museums create such situations, where mindful attention allows a museum user to craft, in Kierkegaard's words, a truth that is true for me? This concept—going beyond the information given—comes from Jerome Bruner, as does the idea that we are always in the process of renegotiating and improvising in our relationship with our culture. Similarly, I assume, a faithful person in a fluid world is always renegotiating a relationship with the divine. How might museums create circumstances where users are given opportunities to reduce their confusion, confirm their mindfulness, and articulate their place in a challenging universe, by coming to understand spiritual practices across differences?

FIVE THOUGHTFUL EXERCISES

At the Five Faiths Colloquy, I offered the following five exercises, each conducted by a small group of participants. It was my intention to create experiences where the actual outcomes of the conversations would be less important than the interactions that occurred as people gave attention to the objects they selected. It was this attention that seemed to matter most in the group. Unlike the more academic presentations during other parts of the colloquy, the exercises permitted participants to make choices, to speak their most naïve questions directly, and to share their perceptions with each other. Each exercise was designed to avoid "correct" or "incorrect" responses.

In other situations, these exercises might assist others (and not only the conferees) to stimulate the conversational language needed if we are to establish a fearless faith vocabulary. It is useful to remember that these exercises were created for an adult group of scholars, faith leaders, and educators. However, it seemed that even these specialists were drawn to the quality of the collected objects, and eagerly addressed the exercises as learners, not as experts. The Ackland's objects appeared as new experiences to everyone, and so every approach seemed to have a quality of freshness to it.

OBJECT EXERCISE 1: RESTORING MISSING CONTEXTS

Premise: The museum's possession of an object removes it from original, functional, cultural, and worldly contexts. The presentation of an object can suggest or restore some of these contexts, but not all contexts are equally powerful in this way.

Task: Select any two or three faith objects in the museum. Assume that they have no extensive labels or obvious applications in worship. Approach each object with naïve questions about its possible uses or values. What could it be? How might it be used? What is that carving? From among the several contexts suggested below, your task is to determine which of these contexts is the most critical one for the museum to restore. How might this restoration best happen?

Here are several possible contexts for understanding this object. What context is most important? Why?

- Aesthetic qualities, design qualities
- National, cultural, or ethnic origins of the object
- Place in an historical era, among other objects
- Practice applications using the object in a faith community
- Processes of craft or artisanship in making the object
- Responses of the faithful to inherent sacred power
- Scholarly observations about symbolic values

Do alternative contexts enter the conversation? What knowledge would be useful in determining the relative importance of contexts?

OBJECT EXERCISE 2: LIKENESSES AND DIFFERENCES

Premise: The museum places an object among many other objects, and so creates a problem for the user's attention. We might encounter museum objects in isolation, or in a series, or a set; they may be linked by a theme, a structural similarity, their history and geography, or their maker. Regardless of the museum's efforts to shape our attention to these patterns, we tend to juxtapose and compare similar objects from different places in our desire to think critically about their nature.

Task: Select any two or three faith objects in the museum. What grounds for comparing this set of objects appear to be most promising? What might such comparisons suggest? Among the chosen objects, is one more complex than another? If two or three other objects are added to the set, do the grounds for comparison change?

OBJECT EXERCISE 3: THE INCOMPLETE OBJECT

Premise: The museum's presentation of an object or a text does not assume that the object or the text is "complete." Only our attention, inquiry, or individual observations and expressions can complete our experiences of the object. In this way—by our attention—we construct a bridge from the artifact to the human being.

Task: Select any two or three faith objects in the museum. From your perspectives, what do you not know that you need to know, in order to complete your experience and understanding of the observed objects? What barriers to your understanding are most evident to you? What kind of information would help you to connect them to other experiences of objects nearby? What are your questions about these objects? Is there a pattern in your questions?

OBJECT EXERCISE 4: THE MOVING OBJECT

Premise: In every object—particularly a faith object—we might assume that something powerful and compelling continues to move in the eyes of a believer. Whatever our relationship to faith, we might say that certain pieces impress themselves upon us, resonate and stay with us, show us their energy and power, and remain powerful to us long after we have been in their presence.

Task: Select any two or three faith objects in the museum. Using the concept cited in the first sentence of the premise, what "moves" in each of these things? How can you describe the effect each of these objects has on you? You may wish to use metaphor, analogy, or other figurative language to communicate your observations.

OBJECT EXERCISE 5: SETTING THE TABLE

Premise: When similar objects are juxtaposed, their proximity may create a feeling of connection and resonance, illuminate a common quality as it is shared by each object, or create an unanticipated tension and uncertainty.

Task: Select any five of the museum's objects, each from a different spiritual tradition. If we were to place them together on a table before our group, how would we speak about them? How would we interrogate them? What do their differences in material, size, style, form, or image (for example) imply or suggest to us? What would we do next in order to understand these differences? How might we relate these differences to the faiths or beliefs each object captures?

PROCESS OBSERVATIONS

Following the exercises, these questions were used to discuss the process:

- How would you describe the conversations you had?
- How did the questions change when you moved closer to the objects themselves and spent more time with them?
- How would you revise the questions in each exercise?
- How would you describe your thinking, individually and collectively?
- What lessons does this process offer for our understanding of questions in museums?
- What lessons does this process offer for our understanding of the experiences of museum users?
- What lessons does this process offer for using language to communicate about faith objects in museums?

OUTCOMES

The conversations among colloquists were remarkable and excited. Because the exercises caused them to address objects directly and take risks of personal expression, participants had to move into a different kind of self-presentation and discourse than the colloquy had previously required of them. Faith practitioners, scholars, and educators were required by the process to give up previous ways of examining and "knowing" about the objects before them, because their intellectual skills could take them only to a point at which the unknown began.

It may be that inexpert museum users may react in similar ways, except that the edge of the unknown begins sooner, and their language and experiences may be more rapidly exhausted. Certainly, their language and experiences will be more natural and less filtered by role and status.

Our conversations suggested to me that the transfer of individual attention from object to object seems to involve (1) allowing an object to present itself as a problem; (2) the adherence of the group to a limited set of foci (especially hard for scholars); (3) the awkward fumble and grope of searching for words; (4) the "undressing" of the object from its sacred qualities; and (5) relating this disembedded, less-mysterious object to other objects nearby.

Even in a special group, these conversations about faith objects created a vocabulary that allowed comparisons and questions to be articulated, and new and speakable relationships to appear.

VALUABLE EXPERIENCES AND
FUNDAMENTAL CHALLENGES

In each of the four paired paragraphs that follow, there is a proposition regarding what the museum might hope to achieve, followed by an interpretation (in italic) describing the challenges museums must address if their educative intentions are to be met among religious objects.

Learners require unknowns. It is valuable for learners to have new encounters with the unknown and the unfamiliar. A learner might ask, "How does this object evoke memories? What about this object or experience is unknown to me? What do differences between religious experiences mean? How do we refresh past knowledge?"

For museums, the challenge is to assist museum users to move toward and engage the unknown by helping them to rearticulate and reconstruct what they know, or to express what they anticipate about their own intentions. What do you know now? What do you want to know or become as a result of your thinking here? The personal nature of museum experiences implies that learning that follows our own design depends on who we have already become, and what we have come to understand so far. Does the museum clarify, challenge, or build upon the past?

Learners require language. In museums, experiences that may evoke passion—or reconciliation, ecstasy, solace, inspiration, doubt—are private, singular, and invisible. For learning to occur, words are useful and valuable; they deserve attention in museum galleries where artifacts of religious practice are shown. Even the highly articulate learner may find it difficult to describe the faith object and what it means to a private experience. Learners must think of themselves as questioners, and the expression of authentic, original questions can be regarded as the primary experience of an educative museum. By suggesting processes of conversation and engagement, and without imposing its own agenda, the museum can assist in their articulation.

Among artifacts of faith, how do we mediate experiences or create situations for learning authentically—that is, without compromising the integrity and privacy of the user? How do we assist the silent user to express (if only in private) a single critical insight and thereby unlock the possible energies of learning? The transfer of information always matters less than the transfer of awareness and attention, and so it may be more useful to assist the user to articulate excellent questions, rather than for the museum to answer questions not yet asked. What is the situation that best stimulates a learner to ask an original question?

Learners require accuracy, and sometimes correction. Our formative knowledge sometimes obscures our formative ignorance. Fear and confusion, and even simple caution, may tend to close us down. The museum values a fearless openness to thought, and an acceptance of personal evolution as an alternative to ignorance and misunderstanding.

How do we explore our ignorance? How do we express and construct the conditions for our thinking and learning? Unless it is a place of trust, a museum cannot easily anticipate the knowledge of its users, their unknowns, their hopes, or their interests. Gazing at objects used in spiritual practices, some users may readily shut down as questioners, and this can mean a loss for both the user and the museum. If we wish to sustain open minds as an educative practice, we must have conversations with users, to see where they are in the life-course, what moves them to be present among objects of devotion, and what they are looking for outside the museum, as well as within it.

Learners require contexts. The faith object has a purpose, a physical place in sacred practice, and a physical role in a spiritual system or structure, where it is likely to be part of an ensemble of related objects. It may come into service when moments of loss, joy, ambiguity, or crisis create the need for celebration, solace, or reconciliation. In such intense usages, the object is part of an immersion in religious expression, and its meaning is at its greatest. But the museum object exists outside these contexts and the cycles of faith practice. By definition, every religious object in a secular museum is reduced in power by separation from its original contexts.

We might usefully assume every object to have a contextual biography (not unlike its provenance), beginning with its maker and its original context, followed by its place in a situation of use or value. This biography can demonstrate that practices and meanings have come into play in the creation, use, and preservation of the object. How can we understand the multiple contexts of religious artifacts in a secular museum setting? Questions arise: What is the purpose of an object of faith? Is it a physical embodiment of a divinity? An evocation of religious narrative? An illumination of a spiritual tenet? What structure does it document? Is it a tool, or a container? Does it bear an essential message? What evidences will be useful to explain its contexts? Where did these contexts go when the object was collected? Without contexts, how is the object different? How do we recover them? What is the difference between the object in use—the object being held and touched—and the object at rest under glass? What is lost? Power? Passion? Continuity? What is gained? Visibility? Proximity? Comparison? Objectivity?

Whatever its character or function, each object appearing in the galleries of the Ackland Museum of Art captured and made visible to the colloquists the energies of belief. In our most successful conversations, the power of the object deepened our sense of similar energies and understandings in ourselves. But the nature of our experiences and words clearly made conveying our feelings problematic, not unlike any expression of what faith might mean. As a consequence, my final questions in looking at this experience were really the most personal. Among the objects I found most inspiring, I asked, "What was captured here? What is the nature of this capturing? What is the invisible energy moving in the object? Is the religious artifact more like a tool or a container? How does any language capture the energies of belief, or the logics of a religious system? How does a different language, or a stance outside the faith, inevitably fail to do this fully?" Such questions are better asked among scholars of comparative religion, perhaps, but they also belong where they begin, in the museum.

POSSIBLE LESSONS AND QUESTIONS

Over time and with continuous engagement, the mind is capable of weaving multiple strands, telling comparable stories, and grasping examples of thoughts that transcend categories. Especially in terms of its faith objects, the educative museum needs to redefine itself in accord with the mind's integrative capabilities. The educative museum is grounded in service to the thoughtful user—the user for whom change is continuously possible. It aids in the creation of a public situation for learning without requiring the intervention of teachers and scholars. It is challenged to address its commitments to communicating within these constraints.

A useful response from a museum depends on the flexibility and imaginative capability of museum planners, who must be able to understand the stance and experience of the engaged museum user. For example, as the capacity of a user increases, the museum and other cultural institutions might well develop a place to turn, an expansive structure for collaboration with educators for support of independent inquiry. Among objects made to express and practice religions, it is not difficult to see the educative museum as a resource center where specific, comparative experiences of faith objects—and therefore nonsecular values—can be planned.

I believe that every museum needs to ask of itself: "What is the capacity of our institution for supportive dialogue? How permeable are we to other voices? How shall we invite learners to think clearly about the objects we have collected?"

The enemies of intellectual engagement arrayed against a museum user are perhaps impossible to surmise, but I anticipate that first among them is reduction or condescension. In its labels and texts, the museum tends to give too little that is useful. The second enemy of minds in museums, I believe, is the distortion and lofty distance of excessive scholarship. And perhaps the third is silence and discontinuity; think of the mind in midair, entirely concentrated on grasping the next thing, waiting for the trapeze that does not arrive. These obstacles are forms of arrogance. It should be understood that humility in the presence of learners and faith objects is a useful policy.

Consequently, let us imagine that, across all faiths, we may consider examples of vessels, lamps, adornments, decorations, robes, candelabra, texts and bindings, altars, icons, bells, horns and other soundmakers, even the holy places of worship themselves, and how each follows a design and purpose that serves the values and variations of a particular faith. How might we understand and compare one among others? How might we make the object permeable to our understanding? How can we see the instrumentality and passion embodied in the vessel?

Let us imagine that, of the object, we can ask:

- What is its conventional place and use in ritual pattern and practice?
- Who touches the object?
- How and when in the observation is it used?
- What is its meaning in observances of birth, death, initiation, transformation, or other continuities of human life?
- What is its relationship to sacred text or narrative, symbol or deity?
- What is its comparative complexity among other objects of its kind?

Let us imagine that, of every faith—including all tribal faiths—we can ask:

- What is the path of a human being toward the divine?
- Who is the human being who is an adherent to faithful practice?
- How does the deity or the faith "see" the human?
- How do such objects as these assist a person along the spiritual path?

These questions attempt to suggest the value of objects that communicate about faith, especially in secular cultures with strongly compartmentalized areas of understanding—and variable histories in the tolerance of difference.

When museum collections hold powerful objects, it is often difficult to know how to address their power. We may allow the language of art to make them conversational and reduce them as emblems of faith. Religious practices, and the meanings of spiritual objects and artifacts, are not part of our common talk, though religion appears in the news and among our leaders in abundantly political and sometimes exploitative ways. The topic is always hot, the issues are always troubling, and they do not go far away. Politics is often imbued with implications and assumptions pertinent to private beliefs. Although a museum cannot address these social and political implications of faith, it can begin to construct a vocabulary for expressing experiences of faith objects. We know it is possible to do this responsibly and usefully, as we began to do in the exercises described here.

NOTES

1. The Five Faiths Project, led by Carolyn Wood and Amanda Hughes, uses the Ackland's collection of religious art in photography and storytelling workshops, posters, exhibitions, and related programs. This author was invited to participate in its colloquies and in the design of its final gathering. The exercises described here were first presented at the colloquium in August 2002. For information about the project, contact fivefaiths@unc.edu, or see the Web site of the Ackland Museum of Art, www.ackland.org.

2. The Ackland Art Museum, "Five Faiths Project," <http://www.ackland.org/education/fivefaiths/ff_index.html> (4 February 2005).

8

OBSERVING COLLABORATIONS BETWEEN LIBRARIES AND MUSEUMS

Communities and cultures, like learners, need to be challenged if they are to understand what they can do, what they are, and what they might become. There is no more important task for museums and libraries than to seek renewed understandings of how cultural institutions and the lives they affect can interact with each other, how we can act toward each other, and how we might think differently about a future in common. The rhetoric that once addressed the possibilities of the new millennium has come true: the rules and values of the previous century are all worth questioning.

We have so much more to understand whenever our community or society is under stress; our definitions and our anticipations of need have to be revised. In these unanticipated circumstances, our institutions have no choices about our responsibilities to serve and to assist critical thought and human judgment. Our responsibilities in cultural institutions suggest that we should constantly reinterpret our values and organizations, that we can begin to think with others, and that institutional success may have nothing to do with anything any of us can count or measure. If lives do not change because of what we do, perhaps we have misinterpreted our purposes.

When citizens are challenged by their own understanding of order and governance, when they ask difficult questions about what their lives and destinies mean, when they require trust and solace, and when we have no forum at hand to debate essential issues, I think it becomes even clearer that the tasks of a culture's institutions are to assist in the management of human questions, to create fair and trusted forums for self-exploration and self-presentation, and to help conduct the conversations essential to civic enrichment. Museums and libraries should do this together.

After twenty years of thinking and observing, I believe that these are simply the critical things that robust institutions do. I do not question for a moment that collaboration among institutions is both the genius and the future of our essential cultural institutions, the public library and the educative museum. According to my values, a capacity for collaboration (with individuals or with consortia) is the essential characteristic of the strongest of these institutions.

On two occasions, I have served as an evaluator of major collaborations between museums and libraries. From 1991 through 1995, at the Children's Museum of Indianapolis, I observed the original Rex's Lending Center project, funded by the W. K. Kellogg Foundation.[1] Second, from 1998 through 2001, I observed the Art ConText project in Providence, funded by the Institute for Museum and Library Services and the Pew Foundation, where the Rhode Island School of Design Museum of Art collaborated with the Providence Public Library system to support the presence of artists in library-based community residencies. On another occasion, I addressed the collaborating staffs of the Howe Library of Hanover, New Hampshire, and the Montshire Museum of Norwich, Vermont, as they developed small museum exhibitions for rural public library settings. I have lately assisted the Queens Museum of Art as it readies itself for a Queens Library branch within its future structure.

The characteristics of these collaborations hold much in common. The projects are unprecedented and therefore required a careful approach as institutional experiments in processes and goals. In each case the largest challenge is to communicate usefully among planners, and to communicate effectively with partners. Ideas must be restated and re-envisioned steadily, in order to develop them appropriately and flexibly. The value and purpose of each collaboration will affect the programs, policies, and identities of the partnering institutions. Boundaries and divisions of responsibility, clarifications of roles and functions need to be articulated for a balanced partnership. New missions and conditions will emerge, grounded on past missions of course, but no less fresh, engaging, and challenging to everyone.

In Indianapolis and Providence I interpreted my role to include an advisory, evaluative, and catalytic component, almost an advocacy. I offered formative advice as well as interview- and observation-based evaluations of the successes and weaknesses in process and progress. My naïve questions among participants often led them to insights about the adaptations that they had made over time, not simply in relation to the funded project, but in relation to closeness between institutions as well. At times, my task was to make progress visible.

As a result, I have not only attended to the outcomes of these collaborative projects, I have been able to view their evolution from a nearby perspective. I should add that it has been my advocacy for these same twenty years that libraries and museums serve virtually the same values, the same communities of learners, and the same intentions. To be clear: these were projects of a kind I had always hoped to witness, and embodiments of values I had long endorsed.

Many common values inhere among the experiences of museums and libraries. All museums and all libraries are centers that depend on practices of literacy, imagination, and awareness: thinking, remembering, reading, responding, imagining, integrating, reflecting, connecting, communicating, and problem solving. (Schools share these interests also, but often in differing proportion, and under completely different circumstances.) What public partnerships might evolve surrounding these critical activities? In what ways might cultural institutions address these innately human processes and engagements as matters of course in their programs and policies? What must happen between institutional partners before an effective, mutually designed project can begin?

When two institutions collaborate, what becomes possible? A broader audience can be envisioned, and shared information about users and their needs can expand the cultural frame of a community. The use of applied information in the museum and the exemplary value of the artifact in the library can be mutually enhancing. Recognizing that people of intellect and good will can engage productively in situations of complexity and relevance, partnering can change the processes and the contents of the organizations and their professionals. It is likely that partnerships with other institutions—academic programs, health care agencies, faith communities, civic organizations—become more possible as well.[2]

It is not just good and useful to collaborate; it is also responsible and ethical. In my experience, when visible, concerted striving extends cultural institutions to reach thoughtfully toward their publics, the people will reach back to the institution with gratitude and pride, knowing that their possibilities as a community have been extended.

Cultural institutions exist in a community not simply for knowledge, delight, and instruction but also for the negotiations and explorations needed in a contemporary life—growing up and growing through, finding a vocation, reading the best of what is written, managing the brutal onslaught of junk information and other distractions of commercial culture. We know that we must see our institutions as places meant to advance useful encounters and reflections; they make us more functional and more confident as citizens.

If we are strong learners, we also know that there are no easy questions in our lives worth taking on. All of the best problems are difficult, and none of them will end. There also seems to be no end to the permutations among our critical, fire-breathing issues: ethics, politics, economics, religion, race, gender, medicine, community, even the values of kindness and generosity. Every one of them touches every other. We need only read the news to know that these dragons animate the everyday, and that it is a rare day when one of them does not singe our attention, or mark us with its teeth. We need to restore and rescue ourselves, make ourselves more aware and more informed, somewhere.

The permeable borders of our best institutions—the least insular and arrogant ones—are the ways we have of establishing new mutual exchanges, new programs, and a new ease of communication between libraries, museums, and communities. When institutions explore these borders, they are likely to find that they have discovered or created room for negotiations and conversations, and even the vast imaginary spaces needed for institutional change to happen. Information flows into the institution; it changes the place and the people inside it, and different information flows out. When invited and respected, the public will advance its interests by participating in the processes of institutional renewal.

It seems to me that there are three main forms of collaborative purpose; each has an associated basic model and probably multiple variations.

Thematic collaborations integrate museum collections and information resources in ways that stimulate both the presentation of content and the likelihood of independent discoveries among users. (A collection of relevant written materials is introduced to a museum gallery; a collection of artifacts, tools, or specimens is displayed in a library; a special museum, botanical, or historical collection is digitized and made available in both institutions. The successful interaction and collaboration can lead to new planning questions, "What do we share? How can our partners join us?")

Constructive collaborations recognize the mutual value of unified attention when institutions address a systemic or community-wide issue; new structures and relationships are designed to increase public focus and generative responses. (A physical environment for collaboration is emphasized. The museum uses its galleries as new spaces for literacy initiatives; libraries hold public conversations about family learning with museum educators present; museum workshops are held in library spaces; teachers are invited to use human and material resources from multiple partners.)

Civic collaborations address the cultural values of a community, and the issues of concern in a nearby civic environment, in order to enhance wider understanding. The collaborating cultural institutions attempt to develop new awareness, respect, and responsibility—and accord among multiple players. (The potentially divisive characteristics of a community—ethnicity, religion, history, ancient misunderstandings—can become significant themes for documentation, analysis, and explanation, rather than points of division. It is possible that an endangered civility and environment of respect can be recovered through dialogues, oral histories, and demonstrations of tradition.)

There may be other models or ways of understanding collaboration; these three have common approaches emphasizing expansion, restoration, and social change.[3] In effect they are models of the behaviors every community requires. All address the idea of a community as a treasury of cultural knowledge with the potential for exchange and engagement, if appropriately catalyzed by its institutions. For an institution of integrity and care, simply paying attention to a public is often expensive and inefficient, but it is essentially just. At the very least, these models might simply be seen as ways to create otherwise unlikely events for communication and conversation. In an insular community, even the smallest steps can become revelations—or revolutions.

Collaborations require an institution to open itself, and even the robust institution should observe several cautions when undertaking a collaborative relationship. We hesitate to take on the ways and practices of another institution, especially when its record or stance in a community is unproven; we look for leadership, authenticity, integrity, and commitment. We are hesitant to begin an open-ended relationship, not knowing where it might lead. We are challenged by the possibilities of collaboration: we have never done things this way before. We may be vulnerable; we may not succeed; we may require more work or resources than we anticipate. We worry about giving more than we receive. All of these concerns are true and reasonable for all partners. But we should also recognize that none of these things has much to do with the future that is to be created, or with the combined mutual strengths of institutions in a well-balanced alliance, cautiously working through hesitations together. In my view collaboration never weakens an institution or makes it less vital to its users.

Perhaps it is useful to embrace collaboration initially as an end in itself. Assume that all good and useful relationships are founded on something that will become clear—a commonly shared question, a subject matter, or a mutual aspiration. Literacy? Creativity? Problem solving in art, literature, history, science? Let the collaborative agenda emerge. Let the collaboration build itself without a grant as its goal. Let a project follow, not precede, a series of explorations where the new relationship itself is the objective. Begin by attending to communication, vocabulary, practices, services, programs. These are anticipatory to trust and its evolution.

What if we revise our sense of mission as we meet together? What if we find that our institutional self-interest is at risk? What if we come to understand the purposes and responsibilities of our institutions anew, without significantly compromising their foundations or collections? How shall we create nonephemeral situations, nonfragile alliances, noncompetitive relationships? What if we question all our guiding assumptions about what it is possible to do in a community?[4] These questions are part of both process and engagement; I think that the confident institution must ask them as a matter of course.

Here are eight observations to summarize the vital characteristics drawn from my observations of collaborations over time. In fact, the phrase "over time" suggests a separate and most important observation: collaborations evolve. The concepts that follow appear to be modest, but they are truly achievements of tenacity and leadership; they are not qualities that appear immediately, easily, or clearly—and they require periodic renewal.

1. *Any collaborative project requires adaptable, tenacious champions in each partner institution.* Each partner must bring a committed champion to the partnership. The champion is a person who is inspired and ambitious for the success of the project, the institutions, and the community. The great champion will emerge as an ego-free advocate, who places the goals of others before any personal achievement. Altruistic champions make the values of the project contagious through continuous advocacy, energy, example, and demonstration that the shared goals of a project are convivial for all partners.

2. *The community always completes the alliance as an equal partner, and should be represented, at least by surrogates, around the table.* The energies of a community are essential to any success, and they must be invited by continuous outreach and public expression. The institutional partners must also be present in the community, together, in public.

3. *Differences among institutions can be profound.* Unequal assets and personnel, academic preparation of professionals, service vocabulary and patterns of discourse, proximity to the community, experience in outreach and public forums, generosity and benefits to users, assumptions of mission and service, assumptions of public need, pace

of change, and history of institutional innovations are merely some of the differences. These differences are challenging and they do not go away; however, they can evolve and become sources of energy rather than contention. Institutions can change and renew each other; there is a strategic value to collaboration for this reason. Consequently, institutional differences should become critical topics in the dialogue between partners. One goal of a successful collaboration is assurance that the integrity of practice in each institution becomes more robust and generative through the partnership.

4. *The greatest challenges in partnerships usually involve communication.* A responsible individual other than a champion should be designated as the agent or broker for communication, continuity, and follow-through between institutional partners. In each partner, this agent is the advocate for collaborative goals.

5. *Every project should involve and present several themes to its audiences, in both library and museum.* Respect for the learner; diversity among users; service to youth; outreach to community; provision of relevant, usable information; innovations in technology; involvement of staff as participants, volunteers, and advocates—these themes are the real legacies of innovations.

6. *Changing institutions by creating an ethos of partnership is a difficult task.* Most institutions are impermeable to other structures, and territoriality reaches deep into an institution's character. A long-standing project has the benefit of years; necessary interactions can occur over time, and gradually institutions will weave themselves together, think and plan with each other. Change itself might best be considered an unspoken goal, a secondary outcome of interaction. The goal of a partnership might be simply to stir things up, and in the end this stirring (and subsequent cooking) may be more important than other goals. The lasting changes in an institution may be less visible and less dramatic than a funder may wish them to be, and it is probable that such changes are not measurable in any significant way.[5] However, their importance is undeniable.

7. *Steps should be taken to make institutional renewal a visible process.* It is useful to hold open, joint conversations between all members of the partnership, in order to confirm its objectives, examine the extent of the project's reach, and reduce obstacles to communication. These conversations can take the form of public forums, focus groups, or expanded staff meetings. The fluency of such meetings will develop over time. Board members of all partners should be

participants as well, to make the embrace of change evident to participants.

8. *A major innovation becomes a defining instrument for an institution*, because it requires articulating values and taking actions that extend its character and interests; such innovations also require an institution to place the community at the center of its work.

Differences between institutions and their missions will create dissonances; these tensions will require conversations and may never be fully resolved. Perhaps the most important, and somewhat paradoxical, quality of change is the value of the discomfort it causes, and the new thinking required whenever a standing institution bends a bit and takes steps beyond the familiar. Issues are raised, and questions must be answered, as the collaborating institution finds itself in a new situation.

For both institutions and individuals, transformations require flexibility; they cause us to learn about both our weaknesses and rigidities more readily than we might wish. At the same time, such changes also cause us to learn about our strengths. Our tendency is to notice negative evidences and worrisome discontinuities first. Consequently it is important to use the situation of change as a way to redefine what an institution does best, and to assure that our best institutional strengths guide our transformations. In collaborations, our task is not simply *to change*, nor is it *to change each other*, and not simply *to change with each other*, but *to change together, for others*.

A strong library brings these things to any partnership: community trust, mastery of information and its forms, egalitarian groundings, commitment to users, and an understanding of a current and fluid world. A strong museum brings these things to any partnership: a desire to communicate beyond its collections, a sense of connection between the future and the past, a grounded sense of purpose among its neighbors, and an understanding of a current and fluid world. Such qualities distinguish a contemporary institution, one that is worth sustaining and extending through partnerships. These are also among the reasons to see the library and the museum as the community's essential catalysts for change, and ideal partners for the common weal.

At its best, collaboration of any kind should mean that a new, compelling energy has entered an institution's life, creating experiences that can inspire a long, lively, and welcomed embrace of self-renewal and permanent change.

NOTES

1. See "Rex's Lending Center and the information life of the child at the Children's Museum of Indianapolis." In Kay E. Vandergrift, ed., *Ways of Knowing: Literature and the Intellectual Life of Children* (Lanham, MD: Scarecrow Press, 1996), 89–118. The Rex project—introducing a self-contained lending library to Children's Museum users—has now become an extraordinarily successful children's branch of the Indianapolis-Marion County library system.

2. It is useful to consider the potential contributions of academic partners as sources of scholarship, advice, expertise, connection, internships, and community outreach agents. Most academic institutions value and advocate community service; and many university departments (education, history, anthropology, and the arts, for example) have clear contextual ties to the work of museums and libraries. Involvements of this kind may also lead undergraduate students to consider museum and library careers, especially if funding for a few internships has been secured.

3. Cultural heritage digitization projects and other information technology initiatives create an entirely new set of possible project models. Partners in the performing arts, public education, or academic institutions will inspire still others.

4. These questions were suggested by Marsha Semmel, Michael Spock, and Harold Skramstad, in conversation on May 21, 2003.

5. In Providence, for example, a major achievement of Art ConText has been the rethinking of the community as a collection of common spaces, where both the museum and the library can have an evident presence. In Indianapolis, one outcome of Rex's Lending Center was the curation of information as an artifact in the museum, and a consideration of information components in future exhibition planning.

9

WHAT DO WE WANT TO HAPPEN?

A good question exemplifies and stimulates mind and art: it moves a person, or an institution, forward. It implies motion toward evidence and discovery, and toward thinking about implications and inferences. The best questions alter or demolish our assumptions and clarify our purposes. The ability to tolerate and cultivate the question, and all the ambiguities it may introduce, is a sign of intelligence among people and institutions; the will to invite and encourage a public question is a sign of courage and responsibility. It is as rare as it is essential for leaders to express the most difficult questions, and to invite multiple minds to work at their edges. And it is more difficult still to honor and sustain the risks of public questioning as part of the leader's art and responsibility. *Why do we not do this more often? What do we have to fear?*

We know the best questions are not to be answered but to be worked out empirically, performed in practice, and once performed in practice, they are to be addressed again, revised, and then made cyclical in the culture and discourse of the institution. *Why do we work as we do? What do we want to happen? What change should we seek? How do people respond to the change we cause?* When our work performs these questions—acts on them, brings them into speech, breaks them into pieces, reassembles them, and puts them into practice—institutions are given dimensions.

It has always been useful for me to present questions to my audiences, classes, and colleagues, in an effort to bring focus to the origins of our motives and to the motives themselves. The searing question has been a useful way to remind myself—as if others did not do this often enough—what little I know, and how much more I am required to learn, and how much better I ought to learn it. I teach in a university, and every day I think the university (and by this I mean everyone in the university, paid by the university) ought to ask, *What kind of institution do we wish to be?*

A big and not-so-simple query, but it seems to be a worthwhile consideration, even when more immediate and mundane policy decisions are on the institutional table. But then, perhaps there is no more important question on an institutional agenda than this one, *What kind of institution do we wish to be?* It is precisely by thinking of the mundane and the everyday that our identities as actors in our institutions emerge, and our intentions as professionals clarify exquisitely. This is the moment for big and not-so-simple questions.

What are the institution's purposes? How do we understand its users? What kinds of growth does the institution want to make possible? How do we want the world of the user to change? These are questions that I would turn to immediately if someone were to ask me, *What kind of information should we give to a person as she walks in the door? What should our organizational map look like? What instructional programs should we create?* I would respond, *What kind of institution do you wish to be?*

In cultural institutions, the mundane is always about guiding values and intentions, and how the institution interprets possibility. When the thinking is not mundane, when an institution really needs to do intense and fundamental research in order to document its quality, impact, audience, or needs, central questions for the heart of the institutional body are necessary. They will guide the methods, depth, and extent of institutional research. *What excellence do we strive for? What questions must we ask?*

The following list of questions was generated for use with a museum staff as they considered the need to conduct a self-study. I believe they can be used in any cultural institution, with slight adaptations. As a consultant, my work with such questions is first to pose them and explain them; the structure that follows also organizes them into domains with some overlap. The unknowns suggested by these questions, while they are not arcane, seem to make clear that the simplest questions, say, about attendance and use, are not so simple.

In conversations among institutions, I also strive to grasp and communicate the priorities such questions represent, and then I try to translate them into the situations and methods that will allow the expression of appropriate responses. I attempt to make sure that the questions themselves do their first work in evoking an institution's values and intentions; then we move to the response. Great—that is, challenging and difficult to answer—questions are provocations for self-evaluation; in some cases their persistence and guidance will appear as part of an outcome. A question can be so powerful that its very asking is a kind of indicator or moment of pause, a reminder of larger things. My questions are offered as instruments—as ways for institutions to pause, to begin thinking of themselves as having made decisions, and to understand their decisions as communications of their values and definitions. These questions are not to be answered quickly; they are best when they simmer over low heat. In these situations, answers are not as important as we have been taught in schools, or on tests, or when we are sworn to be witnesses. It is possible, in fact, that answers will distract us from the questions and their instrumental, ethical place in our work as it evolves.

Does this institution have a product? What is that product? Is the product a vital product among its users or its community? What need does it fill, what is its cost, and what is its benefit? In regard to this product, how does this institution produce it? Is it manufactured, as in a factory? Is it evoked as in a place of ceremony or worship? Is it taught?

Does this institution perform a service? How, and whom, does it serve? What would not happen in this community without the service? What does the service make possible? In regard to this service, how is this institution like or not like a school, or a hospital, or a library? How is this service offered and accepted by its users?

Responses to these questions are valuable in two ways: they assist institutional self-definition, and they are stimuli for discovering where and how thought and communication flow in a structure of human relationships. When working in museums and libraries, I care about the processes of response such questions educe. I use them to observe how readily a group of professionals can look up from their desktops and communicate, but I also want to see if they can express the possibilities of the institution. I know that responses to these questions are also expressions of their own possibilities within their institutions. *What can we be? Where does our excellence lie? What do we strive to become? Among all our possible acts and designs, what is most promising?* I always hope to find that people are thinking about these questions as guides, every day.

I want the contemplation of such questions—by challenging our convenient thoughts and language, and by being too large for any single person to command—to communicate the idea that the character of an institution results from an ensemble of beliefs and believers expressing themselves; that order and consistency are less important than a coherent belief in the possibility of emerging excellence; and that nothing is more useful than our focused conversations. I also hope to suggest that an institution can successfully embrace an array of allegiances, and even tensions, as long as its character is strong and its conversations continuous. But these allegiances and tensions must be on the table, if an institution is going to understand its energies. An institution's formative questions cannot abide indifference. *What do we do for the human beings we serve? What is our nature and purpose in a democratic society? What do we want to happen? What do we most need to know for our own best possible future?*

We require these questions or other devices in order to break through conventional thinking and unspoken assumptions, the routine qualities that often entrap our practices and compromise our choices. Unless professionals are defining a cultural institution in their own words, its identity as an agency is unclear and it cannot become an open, unfinished, evolving structure. Good practice evolves; the best practice always wants to become something more than it is.

An evolving cultural institution asks these questions. What are our needs? What one of them will make the greatest difference to our institution? What need must our institution address first? Do we require:

- More extensive outreach?
- Stronger instructional programs?
- Different public services?
- A more engaged and active local community membership?
- Greater evidence of inquiry and scholarship?
- Greater evidence of response to everyday questions and issues?
- Greater evidence of adult presence and adult learning?
- Greater evidence of young adult presence and learning?
- Greater evidence of children's presence and learning?
- Greater evidence of racial and ethnic diversity among audiences?
- Deeper and more extensive financial support?
- New collaborative partnerships?
- An evaluation of our professional practices?
- A clearer understanding of our reputation?

What kind of knowledge will assist us? What would be useful to know first?

- How much do audiences know about our institution?
- How accurate is audience knowledge about our institution?
- How often do people use our institution?
- How long do they stay?
- How frequently do they return?
- How accurately do they understand our mission?
- How comparable are other available institutions?
- How rich are our collections in relation to user interests?
- How diverse is our audience?
- How responsive are our services?
- How useful are our relationships to schools?
- How pertinent is our message to our audiences?

When we look at ourselves, what do we want to understand first?

- Our strengths?
- Our weaknesses?
- Our impacts on users?
- The educational aspirations of our users?
- The opinions of potential-but-not-yet-present audiences?
- The opinions and ideas of our staff members?
- How the institution is used in ways we don't see?
- Demographic data on users' educations, incomes, experiences?
- Descriptions of nonusers and their reasons for being scarce?
- Possible changes to be considered in our practices?
- The opinions of users on our services, collections, programs?
- The opinions of members on services?
- The opinions of experts about our options and plans?
- The questions our users would ask of us?

In what parts of our institution do we need to understand the most about ourselves?

- Public services?
- Public programs?
- Public events?
- School and educational services?
- Institutional environment?
- Institutional culture?
- Qualities of space and environment?
- Memberships?
- Development?
- Collections?
- Building design?
- Information provision?
- Public perception?
- Organization structure?
- Administrative divisions?

What kinds of data will mean the most to us?

- On-site survey data?
- Off-site survey data?
- Unobtrusive observational data?

- Telephone, online, mailed surveys?
- Nonaudience focus groups?
- Community focus groups?
- Member focus groups?
- Underrepresented member focus groups?
- User focus groups?
- Staff focus groups?
- Advisory board opinions?
- Financial data?
- Observation data?
- Comparative data?

Who can answer our questions best? Whose experience is most informed?

- Users?
- Nonusers?
- Scholars?
- Professionals?
- Educators?
- Students?
- Staff members?
- Consultants?
- Outsiders?
- Staff members?
- Members?
- Former members?
- University faculty?
- Community?

What will the evidence be compared to?

- An existing standard of excellence?
- Data from comparable settings?
- A statement of mission, standards, goals, and objectives?
- A current definition of service population?
- Dimensions of the collection?
- Previous user information?
- Previous visitor attendance data?
- Measurable collection goals?
- Institutions elsewhere?

- Alternatives to current practices?
- Practices and values in other nearby institutions?

What might our inquiry lead to?

- Changes in service objectives and plans?
- Changes in organizational structure?
- Changes in communication plans and mechanisms?
- Changes in educational strategies?
- Changes in physical space?
- Changes in professional staff?
- Changes in nonprofessional staff?
- Changes in priorities?
- Changes in practices?

How will we consider change?
How will we address differences in our opinions?
How will we define the change we need?
How will we implement change?
How will we know we have changed, as we must?

At least, these are the ways I would begin to frame the most important unknowns that a cultural institution holds about itself. For each question, even the smallest, there are ways to ask, ways to break through, to combine research tools and practices, ways to gather data, and ways to conduct observational and unobtrusive studies, or studies of traces and available data. We might ask everyone—trustees, collectors, educators, volunteers, security and service staff—to notice evidence and think critically about what we are and how the place is experienced now. We might conduct surveys across communities and among specific populations. We might gather and collate and reduce the data until they tell us how to respond to the questions we began with. All of this can be done, and it can become part of an institution's regular self-monitoring.

But then I also ask, *What if? What if this is not enough?* And I wonder a bit about the kinds of questions we might ask under different assumptions, from the perspective of individually shaped experiences, from the perspectives of users. *What if we were to define every cultural institution as collaborative, a mutual creation of its users, its leaders, its professionals, and its board? How could this be?*

What if the institution's purposes are to engage intelligence, cultivate observation, and extend cognition? How does the institution require people to think their way forward into a challenging place and then think their way back? How does this cultural institution challenge its users to think beyond existing limits? How does it lead to critical thinking, or to something we might call a critical imagination?

What if the institution is about hypotheses and questions, going beyond our everyday boundaries and assumptions? What if the intention of a cultural institution is to create a challenge, or explore a problem? What intellectual dangers and risks can the setting support or embrace? What if its experiences contain moments of insight and understanding that last in memories for years? What causes these memories to occur, and to last? What if the most important learning people experience here will occur while reflecting about experiences and discoveries after leaving the institution? What differences can such experiences make in a life—and under what conditions are such differences made? What do such experiences generate in a user's life?

What if the institution is a mystery to its users? How clearly can the user see what has been brought here and how has it been organized? What is the design or plan of the collection and its presentation?

How does the collection encourage the user to think and decide? How do provocative questions happen here? How does the environment assist questions to grow and evolve?

In how many ways can the collection be generative? Where is its center? In what ways is the collection alive? In what ways is it in motion? How does it flow from idea to idea? How is it challenging to our experience? How is this environment about a living system? How does it keep itself in motion? What still-evolving knowledge does it influence today?

What if the institution's purpose is to generate new questions and conversations among its users? On what will such questions and conversations depend? Trust? Inspiration? Scholarly authority? Wonder? Imagination? Complexity? Intelligence? Generosity? If the institution were not present, what conversations would never occur?

How does the institution contribute to literacy? How does it encourage reading? How does the institution contribute to imagination and creativity?

How does the institution address aspirations and planning for further experiences? How is the institution about courage and imagination in pursuit of knowledge?

How does the institution address these continuing critical issues of cultural and civic life?

- *Race, the unhealing wound in American culture.*
- *Competent and inspiring education; the intellectual and emotional experiences of children; the health and safety of children.*
- *Cultural ethics and inequities.*
- *Anti-intellectualism; fear of complexity and ambiguity; reductive testing; the desire for amusement.*

- *The isolation of people from each other and from other cultures, both American cultures and international cultures.*
- *An aversion to public questioning, dissent, or critical thinking.*

What if this cultural institution were to address the ways that people can renew themselves in order to become more competent learners, more active participants in their own lives? How would the institution do that?

What if an institution's purpose is not the transmission of content and information, but to assist reflection and communication, and—in view of the challenges that surround communities and cultures—to assist learning and self-renewal? What more does our institution need to address in order to enrich learning? What if we thought about this institution as an instrument of individual change? How does this institution change lives? What if it could make our users stronger, more confident, more fearless in the face of questions?

This essay contains 275 sentences; there are 218 questions among them. It is possible to respond to every one of them—not to answer each question, but to begin the thinking that each requires, to develop methods and techniques for gathering evidence, to consider priorities and possibilities among them, to find informants who can respond usefully, and to do this all in public. Our questions awaken and nourish our strong, intuitive reactions, our desire to find the best in ourselves, and to lead ourselves toward the best response.

What if the processes of inquiry could demonstrate the promise of the institution to its community, and increase understanding of the aspirations that reflective people nurture as they live and think? What if cultural institutions were to do that?

10

HEROIC LIFE, LEARNING LIFE

> It came into him life; it went out from him truth. It came to
> him short-lived actions; it went out from him immortal
> thoughts. It came to him business; it went from him poetry. It
> was dead fact; now, it is quick thought. It can stand, and it can
> go. It now endures, it now flies, it now inspires. Precisely in
> proportion to the depth of mind from which it issued, so high
> does it soar, so long does it sing.
>
> Ralph Waldo Emerson, "The American Scholar," 1837[1]

When we look at ourselves in any mirror, we are likely to see that we are sometimes designed by the accidents that happen to us, and sometimes designed by the problems we have to solve for ourselves. Whim and construction, two opposites, build every life. I find myself asking questions when I read the newspaper; I think about the information that comes to me without my asking, every day. Is it whim or construction? Accident or design? What am I to think of this? What am I to make of this? Who will help me to think of this? What is it possible to understand? What is there to grasp? Feeling powerless, I ask, What can I do about this knowledge? How are we to think when our worlds are in motion and far from control?

We have few places in American culture for thoughtful learners to understand the challenged common life we are leading together into the future. We share few reflective spaces or open forums, even though our journey is all the shared fortunes, all the open works of our lives and our culture. There are few places for thinking critically, for revising our thoughts in the safety we need. For want of such places, we often do not change, though we might wish to, or though we might need to, in order to become different and stronger.

Our cultural institutions comprise the few open places that exist for us to cultivate our experiences and ideas, to try out our voices and questions, and to find something useful that we need. They sell us nothing, and they rely on our hopes and promises.

When we think about libraries, we have to understand that there are few other places to turn for fair, uncompromised information; to practice risking, acting, and thinking among unknowns; to learn in a nonjudgmental setting; and to move ourselves toward the personally crafted truths we require in order to live one life with integrity, purpose, and success. When we think about museums, we have to understand that there are few other places where we have direct access to objects of art and skill, or to arrangements of parts in a natural system, or to the artifacts and documents that support the narratives we reconstruct, in order to recover the stories lived by our predecessors. There are no other places where our minds are freely proven in the exercise of their inherent breadth and depth, where thinking and learning are the entire purpose of what we do.

Without such places, I believe that we can be subject to despair and fear, and our powers and strengths as citizens and self-explorers are at risk. For those who are devoted to the exploration of knowledge and possibility, the diminution of such collections would have a chilling impact on our identities and imaginations, which must always be fearless, and fearlessly supported.

As though dreaming, we often find ourselves in deep need, isolated and feeling somehow outside the known or familiar order of things, and unable to feel that we have a hand in designing authentic lives. When we are challenged by our weaknesses, or by thoughts of *what might have been*, we tend to go where we are nurtured, confronted, and sustained, places dedicated to the intellectual rescue of people from the abrasions of their times and everyday experiences. I see the creation and sustenance of such places as heroic, restorative, and essential.

Against the circumstances of mindlessness and intimidation that increasingly pervade and compromise mainstream culture, we must become advocates for this heroic work among learners, and strive to practice it ourselves. Emerson said in 1837, "The mind of this country, taught to aim at low objects, eats upon itself."[2] In our cultural institutions, we can observe a form of heroism that acknowledges what it means to learn, and summons the integrity that connects acts of learning in one life. There is no other place in our world where a thinking public can address its differences in experience and reach to meet its needs for critical thinking.

This work occurs *among* others, *with* and *for* others, in the flowing situations of life—in situations of need, risk, and desire—where people need to feel safe and certain as they move forward. The heroic work means growth: learning and talking about what we have learned. It means acting and thinking while resisting the temptation to judge. It occurs in the presence of something unknown, something we sense to be important and valuable, but have not yet understood fully. The greatest part of the unknown is the new territory within us, waiting for us to look into ourselves.

Heroic work is done in museums and libraries by people who demonstrate that inquiry is possible, that change is possible, that something more is possible, that there is an idea, an insight that might change all our thinking if we could simply find it. *This is possible*, such work says, *what do you think of it?* The library or museum represents a place for everyday heroic thinking, and an advocacy that encourages us to think critically and reflectively. It offers strategies and behaviors that will go beyond the moment to serve future inquiry; it teaches asking questions, studying evidence, assuming nothing. Such work is heroic because it rescues minds and energies otherwise lost in an undertow of intellectual indolence and exploitative commerce.

When a cultural institution aspires to become a great teacher, great things become possible. *Trust* is generated between people; our attention is drawn out of us and it begins to pour toward beings and objects in the environment. This regenerates the ideals and values known collectively as *integrity*, the wholeness and strength of mind that lends a quality of authenticity to the learner in process. *Possibilities* appear among an array of all the possible; the learner becomes identified not for what defines the present, but by what expansive thing might happen next. *Openness* appears—the willingness to consider and pursue alternatives to the everyday, keeping our work from closing in order to think once more through the evidence. This openness becomes a source of radiance and energy itself.

It is clear to every conscientious agent, helper, educator, curator, and librarian that the qualities of trust, integrity, possibility, and openness flow back from the learner to inform the helper as well. Both the learner and the agent are defined by such reciprocities. Nel Noddings writes, "Kierkegaard has said that we apprehend another's reality as possibility. To be touched, to have aroused in me something that will disturb my own ethical reality, I must see the other's reality as a possibility for my own."[3] Advocates for cultural institutions anticipate the possibilities of new experiences in other lives.

When we see it and feel it, the inspiration flowing from a life that is given and not withheld can generate and ignite a trust in others. Trusting ourselves, we can pour our attention outward, toward others. Fred Rogers said, "Anything we can do to help foster the intellect and spirit and emotional growth of our fellow human beings, that is our job. Those of us who have this particular vision must continue against all odds. Life," the heroic Mr. Rogers said, "is for service."[4]

A hero of the community mind serves, gives, and lives about something apart from one life; the heroic work addresses something elsewhere, in other lives lived. All of us live forward through experiences composed of encounters with change: erosive change, glacial change, explosive change. We construct changes in our own worlds and feel gratified and accomplished. I think we are at our best when we move ourselves toward change, toward something outside and beyond what we know, probing to find its shape and content, aching to find its heart and substance. And we are most heroic when we are able to transfer the value of this process to the evolving life of another person.

By fostering a community where intelligence is going on, where learning and discussion and conversations happen—and where we sometimes find an idea we cannot easily explain, and find that it remains with us, unfinished as our lives remain unfinished—in this way, our task is to find what our world might strive to become, even when it works against itself, as it so often seems to do. This striving world is not about politics, nor is it about accidents or terror or fear, but it is about the great ideas that move us like winds in sails, on a human course of learning, of becoming and growing into the most distant possibilities of one fearless life.

Our job is to define a life not by its fears but by its possibilities. Our job is not to withhold ourselves from that passionate idea. This is heroism, in just one small life. The Dalai Lama writes, "I believe that our every act has a universal dimension."[5] Ralph Waldo Emerson writes, "The near explains the far. The drop is a small ocean. A man is related to all nature."[6] "It is one light which beams out of a thousand stars. It is one soul which animates all men."[7]

If our task is to find what the world is trying to be, where is that world? I believe it is the world in our minds and acts, and in the minds and acts of others, living or striving to live forward. The evidence will be subtle and fluid, connected and living, unpublished, not graven or hard. It must be the evidence of a fabric, something woven through with continuities, connections, structures, patterns—strands woven and daily rewoven through our experiences.

I think that this is the heroic work of museums, libraries, and other cultural institutions: helping ordinary people to transform their lives into stories, ideas, lessons, principles, all involving an identity, a time past, a time present, and timeless human relationships. Using the contexts of a rich museum or library, a person can come to think of himself or herself first as a learner within a single life-context, then as a reader among great texts, then as a participant in an engaging culture, then as a learner among un-finished narratives, a weaver among the loose threads at the edge of our rough fabric.

We live in a world rewoven every day by insight, by actions or moves toward something, amid the chaotic power of experience. Emerson writes, "Without [action] thought can never ripen into truth. . . . There can be no scholar without the heroic mind."[8] What kind of heroism is learning? In what ways is this kind of thinking—pursuing the wide world at hand—heroic work? How is it that, in Emerson's words, "When the mind is braced by labor and invention, the page of whatever book we read becomes lumi-nous with manifold allusion"?[9] What kind of heroism involves such lumi-nous reading?

It is no different from Emerson's world to our own: heroism follows from character; it is a world where "Character is higher than intellect. Thinking is the function. Living is the functionary. The stream retreats to its source. A great soul will be strong to live, as well as strong to think."[10] On what is the heroic character founded? "Every day, the sun; and, after sunset, Night and her stars. Ever the winds blow; ever the grass grows. Every day, men and women, conversing—beholding and beholden. The scholar is he of all men whom this spectacle most engages."[11]

Think of the Emersonian scholar in our contemporary world as the indi-vidual, attentive learner. An observer and organizer of worlds. A reader of texts, as only texts and not truths, which must be privately crafted. An ac-tive self—not merely a receptive one; a questioner, a constructive builder of mind, as if with lumber and nails. The learner thinks of generations, each building itself in response to its own world. The learner lives in a world where the past challenges and evokes knowledge of the present but does not preordain it. The learner is called by his world *to know* and *to know* and *to know*, insofar as it is possible to know. Beginning from a centered self and perspective, original and energetic, the questioning, difference-making, gen-erative engine is the human being, in thought. There can be no learner without the heroic mind.

Every life can be seen as an unfinished promise, an unrealized heroism. When we are thinking with care and responsibility—when we are mindful—we can best live up to our responsibilities: to help our children thrive, to recognize and shun greed and venality, to talk back to the screen, to assure fair and equal chances, and to rescue the learner from arrogance, sham, and self-absorption.

We extend ourselves through generosity and trust, and by how much we have helped other people to learn and understand. We are judged by what we have rescued for others more than by what we have gathered for ourselves alone. I think that we open doors for all when we open doors for ourselves and engage in the dialogue that proves us human.

The world is a difficult and challenging place for our minds to be: it's in motion, always shifting toward something new, toward something different, and even that end is in motion. And everywhere we look we see models of human belief in conflict, the irresolvable oppositions of logics and emotions, the emergence of new variables, and new technologies to advance us further toward the remote. We see new contingencies, new possibilities, new worlds, where we can experience the loss of national order and continuity in one brief but eternal September morning.

Emerson was born two hundred years ago, but we are learners in the twenty-first century. Ours is a world in somewhat more rapid motion. Our conflicts and encounters with change challenge us every day. There is heroic work to be done, but the pervasive contexts of our times are expansive and enfolding: they are ethical, political, cultural, religious, racial, humanitarian, medical, communal. We are challenged to unfold them, but all the evidences of the world around us are linked and inextricable.

After September 2001 I asked my students to address with me the questions I now ask others. *What do we need to know in order to understand human differences? How are we to think, when our world is in motion? How are we to think, when dire knowledge comes to us unbidden?* It seems to me that, among the many responses to the events of September 11, perhaps the least-heard was "To understand, we must learn more."

To learn means to become; it is the purpose of the American learner to become a person of larger capacity and perspective. As I understand the grounding of our nation, this is a conscious intention of the founders; it is why we have cultural institutions and also why we need people who pledge their lives to sustain them. It is why we are permitted to speak and read freely. To learn is to overcome the dread of change, the fear of challenge, the fear of fear. It is to overcome our own mistrust of intellect and self-education, and our dependency on teachers and schools. It is to overcome our small perspectives on immense possibilities, our crippling desire for entertainment, our need for easy solutions from someone else, our intolerance of ambiguity. Our linear, unimaginative, ungenerous, unplayful thinking. Our pursuit of answers, not questions. Our inability to seek help. And to learn is perhaps to overcome the epidemic disease of our time, which is impatience—or is it now fear?

To learn implies thoughts at an edge. Moving to the edge is a preparation for learning. An edge implies a view, sharpness, a risk. Institutions, scholars, librarians, educators, teachers, mentors, docents help us to move to the edges we require as learners, but they cannot do more than help. We must want, in some way, to be inside their minds and values, dwelling, like Emily Dickinson, in possibility.

As it was for Emerson, as ever it has been, all learning follows from passion, articulated in our words as a series of questions—each question in its own way a revolutionary instrument, authentically our own. For this revolution, as it was for Emerson, every learner is grounded in a repertoire of language, experience, and memory. Our words, and what they stand for in our lives, move us to the edges of thought, where we are all meant to be. For a learner, the edges of possibility are everywhere to be discovered. What do we want to have happen to us? What is our heroic service to the American learner now?

The distances between Thomas Jefferson, born in 1743 and dead in 1826, and Ralph Waldo Emerson, born in 1803 and dead in 1882, and John Dewey, born in 1859 and dead in 1952, are less than we might think. There are ideas of the eighteenth century, and the nineteenth and twentieth, which have become our own legacies to carry and articulate in the twenty-first. That we have no Jefferson, nor an Emerson, nor a Dewey of our own should remind us of our own personal obligation to transfer that legacy, or it will be lost entirely to our time and our children's time. There will be no more Jeffersons, but he will always be in the room whenever citizens gather to think together.

In communities near my home in North Carolina, guided by librarians and other strong readers, thousands of citizens have taken up books and conversations about them that strengthen and expand their awareness of the unspoken beliefs and experiences in their communities. Under rubrics like "One City, One Book" (Greensboro), "Wake Reads Together" (Wake County), and "On the Same Page" (Forsyth County), people have read and discussed *To Kill a Mockingbird, I Know Why the Caged Bird Sings, Fahrenheit 451, Wolf Whistle, A Lesson Before Dying,* and others—not one of them an experience to be undertaken lightly anywhere, but especially not in the American South.

The embedded issues such readings and conversations send streaming through workplaces, public schools, civic associations, houses of faith, correctional facilities, adolescent service programs, and professional groups are unlikely to have been expressed in public before. "Telling the truth with compassion," in Greensboro's phrase, changes a community as it changes readers. It creates a middle place, a place that is not a place, for the telling to happen, a ground for common experience without a certain outcome.

Speaking to librarians in Greensboro recently, I wanted to make a point about the complexities of communities holding diverse immigrant populations. But I suddenly stopped and said, "But of course you all understand this, having read together Mary Pipher's book *The Middle of Everywhere.*"

When we read together, we know together and gather lessons together. Deep, socially instrumental reading is one example of the way an institution can express its promise to the common cognitive lives of its citizens. When we come together as readers we can freely speak our perceptions through our own lived experiences; we can bring our entire selves and memories into the room, and when we read together, we take up residence in that place that is not a place, where we are when we imagine ourselves across another dimension, into possibility.

Whatever we might read, there is work for us to do in helping to inspire the American learner as a reader who will act in the Emersonian sense, reading and speaking with heroic passion. My suggestion arrives at a moment in our national life when we all may believe ourselves acting to create a stable and strong society—and half of us will cast a vote quite opposite to the other half. Therefore it is our task to create the public forums we need, to pose the difficult questions and set the rules for our conversations to follow. In the course of this, we all might discover that there is a learner present who has arrived at this time and place as if by design, ready to listen to others with care, and to speak as though laying a path of words into the future.

When we meet that learner, we will find a person who is open, dynamic, balanced, reacting, becoming, but also cautious, tentative, unformed. One who, learning, seamlessly mixes acts of adaptation, responsibility, improvisation, and reimagination—and the blessing of uncertainty. What is the meaning of difference? How shall we tell when we have become different?

For such growth of knowledge and perspective to take place, a reinterpretation, a reinvention, and in some ways a rediscovery of trust in cultural institutions must happen. The intellectual problem of our time may not be about withered brain cells, overpraised technology, vapid television, a wealth-driven economy, or a test-driven education—since it is difficult to know exactly which of these has damaged our common experiences the most, and which most needs our attention and repair.

The intellectual problem of our time is the larger and always constant need for self-discovery and rediscovery and self-recovery through conversations across every age of learning. These are conversations of which each of us is capable. If our institutions do not rescue the learner through talk and hope, the learner will be lost. This is the time to look for and to understand the mind's great rescuing energies in every one of us. I hope that Emerson would agree: to advance our lives, we must reimagine them continuously and heroically, rescuing others and ourselves until we end.

NOTES

1. Ralph Waldo Emerson, "The American Scholar," in *Selections from Ralph Waldo Emerson*, ed. Stephen E. Whicher (Boston: Riverside, 1957), 66–67. This essay is written in an Emersonian mode, and was originally titled "The American Learner," after Emerson's great oration, "The American Scholar" of 1837.

2. Emerson, "The American Scholar," 79.

3. Nel Noddings, *Caring* (Berkeley: University of California Press, 1984), 14.

4. Retrieved on December 9, 2004 at http://www.curezone.com/forums/m.asp?f=173&i=712.

5. His Holiness the Dalai Lama, *Ethics for the New Millennium* (New York: Riverhead Books, 1999), 161.

6. Emerson, "The American Scholar," 78.

7. Emerson, "The American Scholar," 76

8. Emerson, "The American Scholar," 70.

9. Emerson, "The American Scholar," 69.

10. Emerson, "The American Scholar," 72.

11. Emerson, "The American Scholar," 65.

11

MEMORY

THE PERSONAL PAST IN THE PUBLIC SPACE

Every life writes a text with hidden pages, some unreadable even to their author. But there are illuminating moments in museums, found in no other places, when such pages become visible and their messages become clear. An object suggests an idea we have not encountered in years. An exhibition holds a theme that touches our forgotten schooling. We see an image of a past time and place and we recognize it as the experience of our family, or of a family like our own. The challenge for an educative museum is to create a situation where communication is valued and context invites and illuminates memory without compromising the authenticity of content.

We are still at the edge of the twenty-first century, and the theme of remembering (and related themes of narrative, reconstruction, and conservation) appears at the center of our common search for an understanding of the twentieth. Especially in the observations of World War II from sixty or sixty-five years' perspective, the *idea* of memory can easily dominate the details of memories. What does it mean to be the rememberer? We analyze the meaning of memory even as we listen to those who recall their experiences of D-Day and the Enola Gay, of Iwo Jima and Dresden. Tensions between recorded history and living memory meet even in presidential debates, and at stake is the ownership and rededication, or perhaps the theft, of the past.

In the landmark example of the Smithsonian's reduction of the Enola Gay exhibition, the idea of a public story surrounded by engaged critical thinking was made impossible by clouds of resentment, and by fear of the revisioning by historians of tragic lived human experiences. Moments of memory were at stake. The most meaningful recognition to come from that sad encounter between veterans and historians must not be lost. History can be seen as *my* possession, as personal as my grandfather's gloves. History can be *my* knowledge and *my* identity—a living relationship defined more by personal integrity and the need to reconcile stark and traumatic experiences than by scholarship. The most authentic story of the bombing may be what people think of it, how they own it, how it has become a part of themselves. It is the story they tell themselves in order to live peacefully with the past, an evolving crafted truth. Memory is as much a manufactured artifact as the cockpit window; but it is made of feelings, and it is less transparent.

We have seen how powerfully a crafted and burnished personal memory can stand among artifacts, assert itself, and demand that attention be paid. Edward Linenthal described this power as the "inevitable tension between the commemorative voice and the historical voice when history becomes the focus of a public exhibit or ceremony."[1]

It is not my purpose to address this event, but to contemplate the value of individual memory to the museum. Controversy aside, there is no more likely place than the museum for the meeting of recorded history and living memory. Ideally, here the reconstructed records of scholars and the crafted memories of witnesses can intersect to create a productive forum. Here multiple crafted truths can be expressed. Here, where memory is respected evidence, a human repertoire of experienced narratives and authentic stories can be told. In the museum, history can be practiced as it is understood by its scholars and held by its witnesses—each kind of knower touching and telling the truth differently.

The crafted memory appears in the voice of the witness, unique and intimate. I think of my own father's World War I stories of biting lice and acrid gas; I think of my mother's memory of horses in a burning barn. For each of them the crafted memory was kept alive to be revisited and augmented over time. There must have been countless other, unspoken memories, even more formative than those I heard. The crafted memory is one we work to keep actively in mind in order to remind ourselves of the story that happened to us and brought us here. We present it to others as a remnant, a trace of ourselves. Whatever its verity as a report, the crafted memory is true in the sense that all caringly constructed narratives hold a truth for their narrator. The crafted memory is recollected and held as a small, carved treasure is held in the palm of the hand.

The meaning of such memory for the museum is not difficult to see. Evoked in the museum, individual memories are momentary mirrors of the invisible life now gone: they inspire an instant of reflection and recovery. When a memory is recovered and shared among companions, the integrity of the observation and the intensity of its personal contexts are transmitted, and these are undeniably alive.

TWO ENCOUNTERS

Memory transcends the bland narrative and the perfunctory label: it can deepen and extend the human presence in things. Here are two encounters with living memory: one is a meeting with a human witness and the other is the discovery of an object that becomes an inanimate witness. Each encounter comes out of the Holocaust.

In 1992, while consulting at the Children's Museum of Indianapolis, I saw for the second time a traveling version of the child's-eye-view of dispossession and destruction, *Remember the Children: Daniel's Story,* later part of the U.S. Holocaust Memorial Museum in Washington, D.C. I entered the exhibition with well-informed understanding. Many books and essays on my shelves, many films and photographs, and knowledge cultivated over twenty years accompanied me; and I had seen this exhibit a year before, in New York City. Seeing it again in Indiana, I reviewed the familiar images, words, and sounds, comparing one installation to another, wondering how the Midwestern eye interpreted this narrative—two years before the story of Schindler's list was well known across America. The spaces were more open, less constrained, and discontinuous than they had been in the New York venue. Here, I felt, one had a better opportunity to know the sense of Daniel's passage better. His family's inevitable transport and fate, somehow, were clearer.

In this setting, several local Jewish guides assisted; I joined one and his group in progress, in the ragged and dim simulation of a ghetto apartment. He spoke of the privations and scarcities experienced in rooms such as this one. But this simulated interior, I thought, could never fully simulate the fear—the grave knowledge of the world outside—that must have been rampant, even redolent, in real space and lost time. We had moved beyond this room, to a space with a wall-sized photographic mural of a camp, railroad tracks, and debris. I was writing in my notebook when the guide—in his late sixties, direct and articulate in his speech, with barely an accent—alluded to the railroad cars in the photograph and to the small humans in the large image. "Look there," he said. "I am one of those in the photograph." And he went on to tell about his job in the camp: collecting luggage and other possessions newly arrived with their owners and then stripped from them to be ransacked for treasures.

He spoke a few more sentences and then said, "Perhaps you have not seen something like this." And he rolled up his jacket sleeve, then his shirt-sleeve, to show a tattooed number just above his wristwatch. He went on to talk more about his life in the same voice. Later in an adjacent photographic study of survivors, I read about him and about his lost parents and siblings. I thought again about what I had earlier felt to be missing in the simulated ghetto rooms—that grave knowledge of the exterior world, knowledge that the boy in the photograph, collecting luggage by the railroad tracks, knew when the photograph was taken. The presence of a witness and the authority of his voice had filled my experience completely.

Talking about this moment later to my students, my voice was unexpectedly heavy and quite unsteady—in fact I had to stop talking about the experience—not with new knowledge of my own, but with the sudden transformation of the narrative as I had experienced it in Indianapolis. I had encountered a dedicated conservator of memory, a man whose exquisite effect had been caringly crafted out of an experienced nightmare. No narrative I had command of, either on my shelves or in my thoughts, had the weight of this encounter. And no exhibition, not even the U.S. Holocaust Memorial Museum itself, could fully capture and present the power of his rolled-up sleeve.

The second encounter is told in a narrative by the contemporary German writer, Erich Fried, "My Doll in Auschwitz."[2] The writer visits the Polish camp in 1967, fearful and uncertain. The night before his journey, he reads in preparation, "as a help against anxiety and against the shivering." In the experience itself, he finds that his reading prepares him to acknowledge and verify what he sees—the "unbearable became for a few seconds almost bearable. . . . I had expected the mountain of shoes, I had also read about it and seen photos." The writer moves on, seeing pile upon pile of remaining possessions, remnants of the dispossessed in Auschwitz. Then his memory is suddenly present in a different way.

> Even more surprising was the mountain of children's toys. I could not remember ever having read anything about it. . . . Or had I quickly wanted to forget it? Apart from that I had children myself, and that didn't make it any easier. . . .
>
> Somewhat helplessly I looked at the pile of toys, partly damaged, partly well-preserved. Suddenly I saw Moritz. Moritz was about ten inches high, red haired, with a green jacket and green trousers. He was on wheels, so that when he was pulled along on the string, he alternately

bent forward and leant back. At the same time he also swung his arms
and legs. It wasn't me pulling him along on the string; I was separated
from him by a glass barrier, but I knew exactly. It was a reunion. Moritz
had been my own doll, broken when I was four years old, but now completely undamaged. As a child I had of course never considered that
Moritz was mass produced. I cannot remember either ever having seen
a second Moritz in a toy shop or in the park where I played. Only in
Auschwitz, more than forty years after my doll was broken, did I see its
double.

From this moment on Auschwitz had a new dimension for me. It was
no longer just the unimaginable other, the completely alien and dead,
instead something strangely familiar had emerged out of the emptiness
and emerged again and again.

The writer then sees the familiar in all Auschwitz objects: he encounters his own possessions in the possessions of the dead, and he rediscovers
knowledge of objects he had lost. "I had never thought about them again,
but now, in Auschwitz, they were old friends."[3] For Fried, this is a breaking
through, as Maxine Greene might call it, a shattering of old forms and old
senses of self: the effect of witnessing on knowing.

From my guide in Indianapolis, I learned that memory is embodied, that it
exists in the person. Offered as evidence among objects, memory has a deep
and disproportionate power to instruct and awaken the experiences of others. Erich Fried's remembrances as a visitor in the concentration camp are
unexpected; they comprise moments when he sees as if into a mirror or an
album and finds a sudden, entire world of intimate connections. *For every toy,*
we think with him, *there is the hand and life of a child.*

To Fried-the-reader, Auschwitz and its traces were constructed as an
interior world of anticipated images, and to Fried-the-witness, Auschwitz
was experienced at a distance—until the encounter with Moritz the doll.
He wrote, "Such details can make possible a leap from one's own fear and
dread to insights and reflections, and even lead to overcoming fear with the
help of what one was most afraid of."[4] To see ourselves, is this a thing we
both need and fear?

Lessons for museum practice in these two stories may be difficult, but
worth stating. Perhaps every exhibition requires a forum, a place for the expression of memories and observations. Through out the museum, apart from
the identification of objects and their contexts, it may be useful to emphasize
the interwoven continuities of things, the threads and ribbons that interlace
artifacts with their human observers. Perhaps, among these observers, there

will be a witness who feels invited to speak up and offer an example from the personal past in the public space.

There is a power in reconstructing the everyday lives of objects through memory and human presence. For every visible thing, there is an invisible context that needs to be evoked, its traces rescued from where they lie silently in human experience.

MEMORY NOTES

Memory, Our Agony

Perhaps we think the past is fragile because so much of its documentation is crumbling and evanescent; but we should think of it at all times for what it can be: potent, dramatic, potentially eviscerating. Its strength lies not only in what we have lived, but more important, what we have lived through. The past carries the possibility of chaos, and it can remind us not simply of how we have lived, but of how we have lived through pain, obsession, error, and all the things contained in the word *loss*. Memory is often our agony. But with these portents memory also carries the possibilities of illumination and revelation, or gratitude and reconciliation, and these possibilities make memory worth our tears, and necessary to relive in ways we can learn from. As I think of this, however, I also think that even the greatest collection knows very little about the possible lives it invites each day, and how each one is unfinished and open, and always fragile in the light of the past.

Audience Is Memory

Audience and memory: each is inexhaustible and infinite, and infinitely variable. It is possible to speak about the topics of memory again and again, each time differently informed, always observing something new, some new trace, some thread. Each observation not only suggests the infinity of remembering; it tells us that memory itself makes the audience infinite. It gives us each our infinitely connected tapestry, still being woven and rewoven every time we examine it. Audience and memory: audience is memory. One by one it is memory and the requisite performances of memory that enter the collection. An audience remembers nothing; one by one, it remembers everything. In the memory collection, the world of the user is perpetually in motion, turning and flowing, and perhaps given value by the exhilaration and intensity of the flow.

Self-Encountered Self

Memory is our self-encountered self. Memory is the narrative that hovers above us and shadows every new event. Memory is evidence we have not been given by another person, even our closest ones, or by our teachers. Memory happens to us, and becomes us. It is the evidence of living that no one else can describe exactly as we can. Memory is our self-experienced self. Memory is us, falling into ourselves, as into an abyss. Like the voice of a poem, without which there is no poem, memory is identical to the rememberer.

The Past Is Today

The reflective user, the author of memory, is never done, but brings a provisional text into our collection, and we help in its revision, sometimes undoing a carefully constructed anonymity. This is our work in cultural institutions, revising life stories. If the cultural institution is to flourish, its first work is to participate in the evolving integrity of the rememberer.

A Construction of the Instant

Like all tentative learning, memory is a form of improvisation, a fabrication based on themes, like a musician's disconsolate phrase or bouncing ramble, unforeseen and unpredicted but never random or truly accidental. If we can use this word, memory is part of destiny. The musician finds what is immediate, inside, and so do we as we remember. The memory is predicated on some moment that precedes it, and, while it may be connected to a stimulus, it comes fumbling forward, retrieved and constructed at the moment it appears. In my experience, memory appears as a vestige of something carried and held close over time. Yet it emerges as a construction of the instant, still unfinished and fluid enough to seep away. These recognitions are exactly what our experiences and personalities have prepared us for, and yet we are so often surprised by their freshness and our own naïveté that we cannot take them in as trustworthy evidences of our lives.

Saying the Names Against Loss

Like the musician, we do perform memory. In Tracy Kidder's book, *Home Town*, a man finds himself in a neglected Jewish cemetery and realizes that the names on the headstones have not been said aloud in generations. He says each name, placing a stone upon each marker. With memory it is the same: it is sometimes enough just to say the names, just to acknowledge the marker, and in all its smallness and enormity, the life it commemorates. Memory—remembering—among the artifacts of a lived life is a way to preserve the life, and so to save it against loss.

Remember the Rememberer

What happens to memory in a world where experience is surrogate, mediated, virtual, unoriginal, packaged and distributed in artless preconstructed forms, designed for us by strangers? How do we act if we want to create a place where users experience profound respect for their cognitive abilities to discover themselves and their deeply held evidences of lives lived? The place that remembers the rememberer invites its users to participate directly in the construction and articulation of its leading ideas, asks them to express a part of themselves in contemplation of something they may never have seen before. The great power of the collection occurs when the human being uses it to encounter the surrounding unknown, and find a place for the human in it. In this way every collection is about memory.

The Opposite of Information

We have the museum, the archive, the library, and the collection all for one thing: to move ourselves forward toward evidence and interpretation, toward crafting our next knowledge. Memory is the opposite of information; it cannot be given to or organized for another human being without destroying its essential nature as our own living and life-bearing thing. Memory seems to me to be a form of momentary play around the evidences of ourselves; play, where the recombination of perspectives and experiences is possible and rules can be creatively transgressed. *I can recognize this in part of myself*, we might say, *but I must play with it if I am to understand its meaning.*

The Imaginative Hand that Unfolds Us

We require a situation where the fabric of play is woven, by stories and instances, around the evidence. In the human life-course, where the deepest evidences lie embedded, only gentle attention will allow them to unfold. In such collections we need to create situations for the grounding of continuous, reflective, mindful, conversational play. Play is the imaginative hand that unfolds us in the world.

SETTING THE TABLE FOR MEMORY

My father, Clifford Wildon Carr, was born in 1896, at the end of the second Grover Cleveland administration, and my mother, Marie Schaible Carr, was born in 1909, when William Howard Taft was in his first year of office. In youth, they both must have been surrounded by Civil War veterans, just as I, born eight days before Franklin Delano Roosevelt's death in 1945, was surrounded by returning GIs, most of whom said very little about what they had witnessed in Europe and the Pacific, just as my father had said little about his war, the War to End All Wars. I did not go to my own war, but kept it at home.

My mother talked about her growing up all the time, from the perspective of an awed, childlike observer of progress; it all happened so rapidly for her, I think she never could sort out what she had witnessed, and what part she played in the drama. Consequently, her childhood was forever unfinished. Her role was that of a first-generation American, the good elder daughter who stayed devoted to her German Mama and her German Papa, who were too busy running a tavern and a restaurant, and favoring their elder sons, to be particularly devoted to her. She nurtured and cared for her younger siblings. In an overweight family, she starved herself.

But she was their most faithful curator in a way, keeping alive stories in which my grandmother survived ordeals, was always the heroine, and overcame the weaknesses of my grandfather. The stories involved my grandmother in a locked and flooding steerage ship cabin on the voyage over, a stable fire where she sought in vain to save the horses, and her immigrant's action in the presence of a patrician neighbor's suicide by hanging. My grandmother didn't hesitate; she cut the dead man down. Each story, as my mother told and retold it, held a moral lesson about her own origins and daughterhood.

My parents lived and grew up among adults firmly embedded in the nineteenth century, configured by a world without widespread electricity, automobiles, highways, radios, airplanes—all just waiting around the century's corner. (My father's English father was born around 1860, about halfway through the reign of Queen Victoria, and likely had parents born under George III. The three of us, my grandfather born in 1860, my father born in 1896, and I born in 1945, cover a span equal to four or five more normally procreative generations.)

I like to think about what my parents must have seen, what their families were like, what my grandparents must have known, how they lived every day, what they hoped for, how they voted, where they found happiness, and what they remembered of all the invisible traces of time on them. But, as we know, even among our most intimate companions, we cannot grasp the traces in memory of another person's experience.

No, I think our lives are not long enough, and will never be long enough, to fully grasp the experience of memory, or to fulfill the concept of memory. It is like neither blood nor bone, yet memory forms us and flows through us just as bone and blood do. Memory, we might say, is what we momentarily restore to the present in our own voices, in the presence of some evidence that suddenly compels us to speak—as though we were in therapy or on the witness stand—and if we don't speak it, as truly as we can, we cannot move forward, toward integrity in our lives. We say, "I remember" but then the story we tell ourselves is a version of our experience, more like fiction than truth.

What does memory mean in our cultural institutions? What does experience mean in a history museum, if the practice of history fails to touch the privacy of memory? What do our inquiries in cultural institutions mean if they do not evoke and challenge and confirm or disconfirm our intuition? What does it mean in an art museum, if we think our task there is to replace what we feel with what we are told to feel, or with dim details we never needed to know? What could a more human touch mean in the library, helping us to feel strongly grounded in our own lives, and our possible lives, as adults? What might the value of memory in museums, libraries, and archives become, if we simply learn to think constructively about it and design a practice that thrives on connection and narrative? What does it mean if the experiences of our cultural institutions lead to nothing recovered, nothing expressed, nothing spoken?

It means that we make nothing happen, because what we want to make happen is exactly that: recovery, expression, and language. We want people to remember and speak. For this to happen, we have to work to create situations of trust and circumstances where memory can be spoken, and where articulated memory can make a difference to experience.

I always ask: *What does it mean, to be the rememberer?* In the most important sense, it is to be the artist and the conjurer. It is to play with evidence, and tell its story, engaged as we should be in our craft, the play of memory and possibility. If memory is to help us learn and change, it should explain the choices made before we were born, the situations of life we entered, the structures of family and community, the passions of history and politics, the economics, the duties of a nation at war and at uneasy peace.

Our parents grew up in contexts, lived with and were formed by their own parents, endured their own wars and lived up to their own responsibilities. They transferred to us—as had been transferred to them—patterns of thought and personality that play out every day in us. We take on life using the terms and perspectives given to us long before we could ever have understood the implications of the gift. When I pause for a devastating moment in a museum, or explore the unexpected possibilities of connection and understanding in libraries, I am working like a poet with the open text of my experience as it has been given to me, and as I have created it, hoping to find myself.

The play of memory in its most important sense implies something that must be vivid to us: motion and structure, improvisation amid the rules, the invention of contexts and narratives. Play is a game-like drama, performed without the arch or curtain. It is the fabrication of our own heroism, and the rescue of ourselves from the past that is unknown to us. We gather data and we play with it. This, I think, is what we engage in when we remember: we try to find a pattern in it, we seek and even improvise to fill the vacancies, and when we remember, we speak in stories. We create a structure, a timeline, a sequence, a passage, a line.

Or we spin a fine strand. We make something connect to something else. We could begin with the idea that we are always weaving and connecting everything. As we stand before the childhood doll or the battered teacup, we may recall our feelings—the weather, the light—at a specific moment in our experiences. And then we will tell the story we remember, and what we remember is all a form of play, a kind of improvised performance, not just a game but a drama as well. And then another person tells a parallel story, or we find a photograph of that teacup in a hand, or another doll we had forgotten, and the drama adds a dimension, perhaps another act. Every life contains a constant performance of memory—and it is always an improvised performance, summoned to the table with the arrival of some foul or fair breeze through an open window. Something happens, and we remember another thing, and we perform this memory unexpectedly, almost uncontrollably. That too is the play of memory, when the past we thought we had lost or left behind, enters the room and sits in the next chair, making us silent.

Memory arrives every day. Memory drinks milk at the kitchen table. Memory goes into our old bedrooms and pokes in the closet. Memory sees our toys and books. Memory has a doll. Memory shows us our first bike, our first pet, our grandparents' deaths. Memory goes to camp. Memory goes to our school, takes the bus, sits in our classes, takes gym. Memory falls down, gets a bloody knee. Memory eats our lunch, plays catch. Memory shoots baskets in the driveway. Memory fails with girls, gets into trouble, feels lonely. Memory plays in the band. Memory goes to the dance, but does not dance.

And when we remember it, we cannot help but attend, one more time, standing against the wall with memory, among the dancing traces of experience.

What are these traces? I think of them as the infinite and invisible pieces we keep to ourselves because we cannot possibly communicate them. When I was about two or three, I smelled the mixed fragrance in my German grandfather's shed, of his empty wine barrels and the damp dirt floor and the honeysuckle on the doorframe. That is a blended trace—none of them is ever pure and isolated—I can never communicate, really, to anyone.

Traces are contexts full of things living and dead; evocative, powerful, sensory artifacts; resonant sensory experiences; the lost patterns and sensations of the everyday; the watershed moments, events or decisions of long ago, after which all things changed; flashbacks; family memories of nothing we have ever directly experienced, but have heard about so often the experience seems to be our own. Traces are shared memories, as between siblings; transmitted memories, things told directly to you alone, for safekeeping; unspoken memories; unspeakable memories; recurrent themes in relationships and families, that last like grudges and legacies. We are always open to these traces, as long as we can remember; and so our stories are perpetually unfinished, just as my parents' story is unfinished as long as I am alive, and your parents' story is living still in you.

What are we to make of that part of history that remains unfinished, but resonant with traces, in us? For me, as I think and read, there are many unfinished parts of history. Surely our participation in American democracy is unfinished; so are what remains of slavery and the national war so centrally influenced by that vile practice. Similarly unfinished, for me, among other things are Wounded Knee, European immigration, Jim Crow, The War to End All Wars, The Great Depression, FDR, organized labor, Manzanar, Auschwitz and Belsen and Dachau, the Enola Gay, Joseph McCarthy, Richard Nixon and Ronald Reagan, Vietnam, Oklahoma City, human rights, November 1963, April 1968, June 1968, September 2001. These are unfinished not only in my life today as I write, but also in the lives of those who may enter the library or the museum at any time. These parts of experience, and others that differ for every one of us, will never be finished in this life, but remain as loose ends in the fabric that clothes American people.

What are we to make of these loose entangling ends, both the human intimacies and the human hammering blows, of history? The myths and the lies. Accidents, disasters, and errors. Coincidences, synchronicities. Character flaws. Contradictions, mysteries, debates. Personalities, geniuses, eccentrics. Undercurrents, movements, radicalism, protests, assassinations. Racism, bigotry, genocide. Alternative readings of documents, alternate memories of conversations. Anti-intellectualism. And of course fear, the intimacy and hammer common to us all?

They are the great concepts of history, because they remind us of its complexities and its effects, and its ambiguities as well as its secrets. We are reminded that history is shaped by a human hand. These are the things that rise in memory, the traces of having lived and deeply felt our lives. We are drawn to the complex because we cannot live a human life that matters while living on the surface of things; every unaddressed ambiguity has a price. I now think that this is a primary purpose of museums and libraries: to remind us of complexity, that no answer is whole, that there is no end to the conditional understandings we need to bring to the past, including our own pasts. Speaking for myself, every day I think about the interactions and combinations of the past, the irreversibility of acts and events, the steadfast laws and phenomena of both the physical world and the mind; I think of the complexities of contexts and the countless chambers of the brain.

Thinking of that complexity that is the past will make it easier to think about the complexity of the future. All our institutions are about the complexity of the future. And that, in some way, is what we might believe ourselves to be challenged by: how to articulate the unfinished issues embedded in the present, and how to recognize in them the unfinished issues of the past. We will not resolve them, but we must say them.

We need to make clear that the world is not finished yet, and neither are we. We will always have something more to become, and our institutions must be part of that. The world is still happening to us right now. I see cultural institutions as metaphors, obviously, for human memory and for the process of keeping and restoring and mining the evidences of our lives. But I would change that word as well, from "memory" to "experience." Our institutions are metaphors for our experiences, for all of American experiences, community experiences, family experiences, individual experiences, lived experiences known only to us until we communicate them to others. Everyone has hidden a story. Where are its traces?

It is important work to tell the story of this experienced life. I think that among the primary themes of our lives still to be articulated in cultural institutions this is most important: the interdependencies of human beings in communities, places where kindness and generosity are practiced, and where we are able to become engaged by the possible stories, the untold stories, in our unfinished world. In the practice of this recovery of stories, our institutions will define themselves as what public memory causes them to become. I would have our institutions be those places where we tell these stories to each other as ways to know that we are human beings, and that we carry our lives as artists do, indelibly expressing our experiences in our work. It is important work to set the table for memory.

I may be talking about our role in civic life and civic responsibility: how we foster discussions and expressions of value in public, and how we enact our feelings and fulfill our promises. To set the table is to take care in addressing our differences with respect and integrity; it is how we should come into the presence of each other, to understand the energy and history of each other. That place, civil society, is where we leave our most important traces, simply by being part of it.

Every museum or library could be seen as a metaphor for the unfinished world surrounding us, and all the untold ways of telling its crafted truths. Our experience is always about the future, but it is also at times about what we recall having once wanted to become, but have not yet found ourselves to be. Our experience is what we carry with us every day as a series of narratives that may, one day, make perfect coherent sense, but on another day may present for our inspiration and awe the great chaotic complexity of human contradictions and accidents, human failures of heart and human compassion, human losses and gains, human constancy and change that is one life. Our history is a series of written and unwritten narratives, a record of memory, and all of them are in play every day, as we imagine the presence of past, lost lives—and as we live their traces in the paths that we imagine and believe to be our own.

NOTES

1. Edward T. Linenthal, "Can Museums Achieve a Balance Between Memory and History?" *Chronicle of Higher Education*, February 10, 1995, B1.

2. Erich Fried, "My Doll in Auschwitz," in *Children and Fools* (London: Serpent's Tail, 1992), 49–62.

3. Fried, "My Doll in Auschwitz," 51–52.

4. Fried, "My Doll in Auschwitz," 58.

12

A PLACE NOT A PLACE

There is an inspired, loving, and deeply moving documentary film—an intimate biographic unveiling, really—called *My Architect: A Son's Journey*, made by Nathaniel Kahn, the son of Louis Kahn, one of America's greatest twentieth-century architects.[1] Kahn died of a heart attack while traveling alone, in a Penn Station men's room in 1974. He was on his way home to Philadelphia from India, and for several days his body lay unclaimed in a New York City morgue. The filmmaker, whose mother was one of Kahn's associates, strives through this work to discover the character and truth of his father, who never lived with him, but who visited often and expressed his love and devotion to the boy, while maintaining two other independent families, each with another child.

As an architect—*his* architect, the filmmaker reminds us—Louis Kahn is visionary and unyielding. Though they are not the focus of the film, his lasting and relatively few built structures seem to inspire their inhabitants to live up to them as places for the possible. Variously dedicated to research, reflection, and governance, they are at once magnificent buildings about magnificent ideas. At the end of *My Architect*, in perhaps the most remarkable space Kahn designed, a huge government capital complex in Dhaka, Bangladesh, a local architect named Shamsul Wares weeps as he describes for Nathaniel Kahn the meaning of Louis Kahn's building in that nation. He says that Louis Kahn's great structure was important because it gave Bangladesh a place for democracy and self-governance to happen. "From nothing, only paddy-fields, [Louis Kahn] gave us his greatest work. Here, in the poorest country in the world, he gave us an institution for democracy."[2] Having the building and its spaces, the Bangladeshi architect says through his tears, meant that people could live up to the idea of autonomy and civic responsibility. The building itself, the place itself, caused something to happen.

When you enter it, a place can communicate and fulfill its own purpose, a quality of occasion that is irresistible and distinct. It is a form of energy; we immediately want to live up to it. The place allows us to experience more than the possibilities of *being* there: it also allows us to experience the possibilities of *becoming* there. It evokes energy from us; we have no choice, except to fulfill ourselves, and the place, as we can. As in Kahn's Bangladeshi building for the becoming of democracy, we go to such places because we believe they give us the power and energy to alter ourselves. They permit us to reimagine the possible, and then they make us bold, able to act to take the possible into some capacious part of our lives.

In Bangladesh, it is a possible society of fairness and order that is to be imagined. In libraries, it is the possible mind and skill to be imagined, or the possible reach toward the unknown. In museums of the arts and crafts, and in science centers as well, it is the possible eye, the feeling heart, the leap of connection, the gesture of the gracile hand—all able to be imagined, because this place exists to hold the possible. In each of these places, especially the library, the place is a place of rescue and notice, where what has been gathered, including the hidden processes of thought and becoming, would under ordinary conditions have been lost, never having been evoked.

Having this understanding of the immanent experience made tenable in a place, we might begin to understand the common promise of cultural places. We find in them the possibility of making differences for ourselves, the astonishment of surprising ourselves, the solace of finding some exquisite hope in ourselves when we had thought none possible.

These important places are also *not* places: they are the *processes* of a community making something of itself. We go to them to experience promised knowledge and experience that has not yet happened to us, and then to consider its implications, and then to grasp how our lived experiences may have made us different. Our institutions are sources of original, generative experience that begins *here* and leads us *elsewhere*, experience that takes us forward, transcending *this*, moving toward *there*.

Processes, experiences, implications, differences: these are always more important than the objects or the information we may find. Their meanings inhere longer and bring us a sense of working, progressive intelligence we would not otherwise have. No possibility can ever be deeply understood without a place to nurture and express it. There is nothing passive here: when we experience an active engagement that leads to something new, it leads us on. The details of our successes will leave traces in memory, but the feelings of anticipation and insight, of having made a difference in thinking, will forever hold more promise. Libraries and museums are cultural instruments for such beginnings.

Our best experiences in cultural institutions confirm an irony: because of what is in them, held in place, it becomes possible to think beyond that place. And another irony: despite the physical dimensions and frequent densities of our places and their contents, their most important holdings are those we cannot see—the interactions, reflections, and interior engagements we make through the objects, tools, and information we encounter. Among these invisibles are the idea that strikes us like a sledgehammer in a dream and the insight that pierces us like an arrow in the forest.

We sign a contract with the unknown when we decide to open and sustain such places in our community: right in the center of town we create a place that is not a place, but a radiant force field of a kind, intended to transform the experiences of those who enter it. And we cannot predict what will happen as a consequence, but the contract means that knowing and anticipating exist permanently among a community's values.

A public space is a "human construct, an artifact, the result of the attempt by human beings to shape the place and thus the nature of their interactions."[3] It is a created sphere regarded by its occupants and users as special and purposeful, and it is therefore never empty because it has been brought into place precisely *to contain* a permanent communal expression of what is possible for learners to learn and communities to become.

Even when we ourselves are not present in it, we know that the public space continues to operate as an open—that is, public, not sacred, not private, not political, not systematic or prescriptive—instrument of chartered community will. When we return to it after an absence, it is again our own theater of action. It awaits our own performances of personal change. These performances require risks and judgments. In this sense, the place is the antithesis of indifference; it can be understood as the community's generative (and therefore antientropic) public agency.

The museum and library as places mirror America as a place; they are the perfecting instruments of the nation's ineradicable public value: the freedom to become.

Great institutions invite great energies. When we anticipate the library or museum it is often with a sense of refreshing immersion in something we cannot clearly name. As learners, reflecting on our experiences and evaluating them, we may be unable to define or even to observe the resonance and flow of such places. We find ourselves thinking of invisible parts of our lives (our needs, memories, and desires) and how we have been marked by our own slow progress in understanding them. We might want a way of saying how we have changed but cannot easily find the words or speak them out loud. To observe the dimensions of change in ourselves as a result of inquiring deeply or reading widely, or having looked at the history of our community, or having played with the possibilities of fresh thoughts, we may find ourselves trying to document the immeasurable. It is part of their design that all great-minded institutions must live with this legacy of invisible effects.

Cultural institutions imply a wide world; they require their users to encounter, refine, and synthesize a robust array of information. But it is a world that comes to us because we have willed ourselves to be present for it; it does not float onto our screen with the mouse click, the commercial, or the fee.

The places will last; our institutions have proven themselves to be permanent and adaptable, and even the sweetest spots on the Web cannot compose the exhilaration of a physical space holding a great collection. The physical is a necessary counterweight to the virtual. While it will always be unproven—and despite the speed and acclaim of cyberspace—the consistency, complexity, and permanence of the orderly and comprehensive library shelf or the provocative gallery will always remain the unparalleled standards for constructive intellectual tools. Unlike the Web, the place is not a metaphor.

The library and the museum embody more than serene models of public access to information; they also capture and preserve the social and intellectual practice that makes all knowledge possible: the provision of surrounding narratives, arguments, and contexts. The gallery and the shelf are continua; knowledge and its practices extend our minds forward and back. Every piece is anchored by adjacent pieces, present to see or touch while we are making choices. These are the conditions of a public practice for free intellectual construction; they do not occur outside these institutions, and cannot occur without an intentional design, often involving dialogue and deliberation. This too means that the institutions of our culture will last.

Yet I know that this will always be true: our institutions are not what they were, and not yet what they must become. Today we may experience a library or a museum and its practices differently from previous generations of learners; now we may find such experiences to be a deepening discovery and exploration of "folds" where each small point of information is simultaneously an intensely specific piece of discontinuous knowledge and *also* a center for connection and transition to other discrete points of information.[4]

This second, connective, generative function is essential to the character of the place and the ethos it sustains. As we explore, we find the fine strand in our discoveries that travels through us alone. We may tie a knot in the strand and move on. Or we may weave it intricately into the fabric we are.

There is no better metaphor. When we work on our minds, we participate in an intricately woven information world where recognizing useful knowledge involves the knotting of threads and the weaving of a fabric. We harvest the filaments, spin the thread, connect the strands, and find the patterns our imaginations will extend. As knowledge folds in upon itself like a blanket, our human practice and art as searchers and explainers is to fold it out.

What these places hold for us and give to us is promise, without which we are more likely to lead compromised and shallow lives. Without a promise of information selected exactly for its community, without human service and assistance to place it into contexts, and without the deepening effects of generative tools and personal conversations, our reach cannot extend into the hidden parts of human experiences, and our lives are diminished.

We cannot think of our cultural institutions for long without understanding that they introduce amorphous, diverse, and unfinished issues to our lives. They move us to a place in ourselves where we are *wanting*, where we ask, and where we understand that as we learn we are not alone. That is also part of the promise: to bring us toward each other in ways that no other institution can do and yet no accounting can ever fully disclose. We stand on the shoulders of giants, of course; we also stand on the shoulders of each other.

In every community, we create systems for having, keeping, and providing what we need most: skill and social strength, health and safety, justice and order, freedom (or recovery) from catastrophe. Police, fire, emergency workers are about safe, fair lives. We also create institutions for service and dialogue—safe, fair community places where we can come together to govern, to plan, and to affirm to each other that:

- We are here, together, more or less permanently;
- We can speak to each other out of our own lives and our need to understand the experiences of other lives;
- We are different from each other in who we are, and what we want;
- And yet we are, more often than not, less different than we think from each other, especially when we understand that . . .
- We are hopeful experimenters, makers, and problem-solvers by nature.

A community and its institutions are often slowly adaptive organisms, civic spaces that do not fully occur and become inspired until we are present in them. We will always need to think of the library and the museum as deliberate, liberating instruments of democracy where lives are freely grown and strengthened by critical thinking and the pursuit of an ideal self.

These institutions embody a common promise beyond the personal, individual promise. They are legacies of the foundations and energies of democracy. To build a public cultural institution is to build an instrument of common possibility and common cause. We make institutions of this kind for a simple reason: we want something new to happen.

We make libraries because we want something new to happen, we make museums because we want something new to happen, we make centers for experiences of craft and art and music and theater because we literally want to make something new happen. And when we are in these centers, the truths we craft for ourselves follow, not because someone has told them to us or told us how to feel, but because we can be calm and unafraid in the extraordinary convergence of imagination and genius. We want our crafted truths to happen. We have these places so we might freely and fearlessly take risks of reading and seeing and thinking, and grow stronger through such exercise.

Increasingly, it seems to me, we find that our task as human beings is to reinvent ourselves and our societies in the shadows of our machines. That is, to find the ways we have left of discovering a personal meaning, of embracing a teacher or model, of exploring a life other than our own, or seeing how the eyes and hands of another person uniquely perceive and capture an image of the world. Wherever we see this dimension of human difference in dance, in print, in fabric, in clay, in paint, and in words, we too are compelled to acknowledge the challenging universe within. We also want to make a difference of our own there.

We require settings that, in their existence alone, stand against indifference—if we want our children to find their own courage to think, so easily erased by time and exigency from our individual experiences. We (and they) need to trust something that extends for more than the instant, something that we cannot consume or dispose of and does not disappear, something that may forever hold an enduring lesson for us. We know that, over time, we can find out what any lesson means. We need to trust in the value of keeping such places, as a student wrote, to encourage gathering, to make a place to dissent, a place where we might go to understand our stories and the stories of others. Another student wrote about our field visits at several museums, "I still need to see the imperfect human story to make anything valuable."

When a community has created the right kinds of institutions, its citizens can discover in themselves what de Tocqueville called "the habits of the heart"—the ways that prove and shape our common character. Through conversations, we experience moments of going beyond the shallow. Through the stories of our past, defining where our community was, we experience a sense of what we have lost and gained. And through the responses we have to the events of our times, we understand how profoundly we are linked by our thoughts and commitments, not only to each other but also to our newest generations.

Beyond places for the practice of intelligent democracy, our institutions are agencies for the holding and keeping in place of our records and our artifacts. By keeping them in a safe place for a long time, we can see them again and again, and remind ourselves of our forebears and what they left us, recognizing that "what they left us" sometimes is imperfect and narrow.

How do we overcome the limits of our communities? How do we counter their tendencies to become private and insular, to build neighborhoods with barriers, and to limit influence to those with power? I offer no answer, except to say that each place is challenged to create a shared sense of what it is, and what it values. What about this place is *our* place? What about this place belongs to everyone? How will we know when we have constructed a permeable culture?

We will discover our answers only when things are happening, and when we have made places for new things to happen: places where words can be heard that help us to live up to ideas; places where we can contribute our gifts to civic culture: our time, our resources, our ideas; places where we can volunteer and assist; places where we can observe and experience the energy of each other.

Our lives have missions and we are guided to complete them by questions that lead us forward. Therefore, every institution needs one thing above all, the strength to nurture our questions, driven by the energy of thought they evoke. To nurture questions is to nurture destiny. One librarian I know in Indianapolis used this question in conversation, to guide her understanding of libraries: "Intelligence is going on here; what is its nature and value?" I try to ask of innovations and initiatives, "How does this cause our community to become more accepting and understanding, less fearful and judgmental?" A museum colleague asks his staff to challenge each other and solve with each other.

Wherever I am in a library or a museum, I ask my questions to remind myself that this place is not a place. What ideas continue beyond our walls? What motives and pursuits do we discern among our users? How well does the situation we create fit the diverse questions, experiences, and interests people bring here? How well do this situation and our work in it advance the educational, social, and cultural values we endorse, such as literacy, reading, communication, health, civic engagement, global awareness, or critical thinking? How do the large themes, social narratives, and public events outside our local world—natural events, wars, explorations, technologies, conflicts, politics, health care, economies, environments—appear in our local setting for our hometown community to understand? What must we strive to create here next? What new questions must we now challenge ourselves to address?

The last pages of Azar Nafisi's wonderful book, *Reading Lolita in Tehran*, provide a text we might easily inscribe on the walls of our institutions.

> I have a recurring fantasy that one more article has been added to the Bill of Rights: the right to free access to imagination. . . . Genuine democracy cannot exist without the freedom to imagine and the right to use imaginative works without any restrictions. To have a whole life, one must have the possibility of publicly shaping and expressing private worlds, dreams, thoughts and desires, of constantly having access to a dialogue between the public and the private worlds. How else do we know that we have existed, felt, desired, hated, feared?[5]

How else can we realize "the right to free access to imagination" unless we have created a space where we might reach toward each other across differences, and help engage with each other in dialogue and argument toward a civil life?

As we strive to become ourselves, we all require gifts of assistance and courage, given from ourselves, out of ourselves, to each other. The community promise of cultural institutions lies in assisting each of us to become that possible person who lives in our interior selves but is rarely apparent, even to us, and yet who wants to ask questions heroically, hoping that one life can matter far more than we too often imagine.

Louis Kahn's heroic building in Bangladesh helped the fragile, complex artifact of democracy to evolve. Kahn said, "You never can learn anything that is not a part of yourself."[6] We need places and ways of exploring the veiled parts of ourselves—ways of reminding ourselves that our most important promises to our culture and to each other will always be hidden within, yet unfinished and open, in perpetual change, always in need of more light.

Here is the mystery to carry away with us: the institution makes so little happen. The library and the museum collect and wait. They do not control or hector their users, nor do they preach or judge. Without even articulating its premise to us, the place not a place strengthens each user to become that possible, waiting person who is always part of our self, living silently in our interior, wanting without fearing, and needing hope in order to continue.

We know that information and communication are forms of energy. We create our libraries and museums as expressions of hope and possibility—and for the different life to emerge when it must, to breathe freely and live more fully, among the many other differing lives in our culture. The human being enters the place, the place enters and expands the human being; and the place not a place becomes part of our own becoming. We inhabit it as we discover it, and its ideas inhabit us as we discover ourselves. We do this for a lifetime, until there is no more emptiness to fill or hunger to sate.

NOTES

1. *My Architect: A Son's Journey.* Director, Nathaniel Kahn. 2003.

2. Cited in B. J. Novitski, "In Search of Louis Kahn," *Architecture Week*, 17 December 2003, <http://www.architectureweek.com> (3 November 2004).

3. Marcel Hénaff and Tracy B. Strong, *Public Space and Democracy* (Minneapolis: University of Minnesota Press, 2001), 5.

4. Hénaff and Strong, *Public Space*, 226–227.

5. Azar Nafisi, *Reading Lolita in Tehran: A Memoir in Books* (New York: Random House, 2003), 338–339.

6. Quoc Doan, "Louis I. Kahn," <http://members.tripod.com/~freshness/> (15 January 2005).

13

INVISIBLE ACTIONS,
INVISIBLE TRACES

Perhaps this is learning: on my office wall, an example of the series, "Homage to the Square," by Josef Albers tells me *Learning never ends*. Box within box, it suggests an infinity of spaces, deepening situations and boundaries expanding, on and on. Learning is a form of continuity. Perhaps learning also has that enclosing, containing quality of the squares: learning is to contain. I also see a sequence in it; learning is both a following and a leading, a succession of squares. Learning follows from the experiences of a human life and leads to the experiences of a human life. Box in box, learning is contained but seemingly infinite.

Learning is what we use to define our world; and learning is what we do to interpret that world for ourselves. That is a professional tension for those who teach or model, or invite a learner to think; we are always following in one way, and leading in another, simultaneously. No one else can discover, define, or interpret this relationship for us: it's all, always, first-hand. Nothing is more personal (to use that old phrase for memorizing) than learning by heart.

It is natural and inevitable to learn some things by heart, or a human being does not survive. We learn to keep healthy, take precautions, seek nourishment and rest, and we reproduce with certain skill. We often do not need to be taught these things. We might also say about learning that much of it occurs against the odds—against the routines, the noises, the distances, the advertising of daily life. We live in a world that works harder to sell us things than to teach us things. *Against* distractions and dysfunctions, we learn. We learn to speak out, and to reach out to engage in our own processes of becoming whatever person we might have been meant to become.

Learning in adulthood is most important when we understand it to be an overcoming of the odds in two contradictory ways. First, our intentional learning involves an activity or an attempt that we *will* ourselves to do, something we design and cause to happen in a particular way, to transform our possibilities. Second, our learning matters most to us when it is an occasion that we cannot predict. Learning is sweetest when it defies or undoes all expectations, including our own. Rather than experience adulthood as a series of ineluctable routines and patterns that hold no adventure, we learn by swimming against the current, and this makes us strong.

Most of our learning is less accidental than we may think; we really have to want it to happen. The accident that teaches us is one we have been prepared to have, the one we had hoped in the dark for. No learning happens to us that we do not somehow need or want to happen to us. And we can marshal powerful personal forces of resistance when we wish to avoid a lesson. Yet we can work like artists to make our learning fit what Gordon Allport long ago described as the *proprium*, our vision of our future selves, the selves we wish most to become.[1] Perhaps this is learning.

Perhaps learning is something we do best when we play or perform, because we do so in the richness of a context, often involving rules and roles that empower us, skills that challenge us, and (at its best) an environment of consistency, support, and cooperation. Here I think of play as a situation that always anticipates the possibility of something unusual and interesting happening in the midst of routine—the triple play, the perfect game, the inside-the-park home run—something we might learn from because it is risky, or unexpected, or because it contradicts the rules, or goes over an astonishing edge. We live for the edge and feel a little blessed and thrilled when we experience it.

Or maybe learning is something we do best when we are deep into our private work, alone in our everyday *practice*, because we do it in a different and more personal context, one where we can experiment, test ourselves, and audit our own lessons, repeat something until it is our own, where we can define the best for ourselves, independent of an audience. When Yo-Yo Ma practices, what does he hear that I cannot?

Or perhaps this is learning: when we do nothing but reflect on experience; when we think of our own invisible transformations; when we think of others living in their separate lives and wonder what they hear.

Decades ago, Eduard Lindeman pointed out that all learning happens in situations.[2] When we act to assist learners, what we do is strive to change the situation by speaking, by using tools and instruments, and by welcoming tentative ideas or words. Some learning will happen in naturally occurring situations, places where a learner might encounter a caring mentor, a willing sharer, a group of responsive soul mates. People will learn, where kindness is practiced and where rules and structures do not interfere with its expression or enslave experiences to time.

Learning can happen in relatively common situations—changing a tire, routines on the job, knowing where to kick the copy machine, knowing whom to call for trustworthy help—or in discovering how to make stagnant time flow by John W. Gardner writes about how Sisyphus would have been a happier person if he simply could have varied the way he rolled that stone up the hill: now levers and pulleys, later a sled, eventually a wheelbarrow or a skateboard, or Nikes, or a bulldozer.[3] A change in situation, tools, or skills would have been good for Sisyphus, without making the rock one pound less, or its lessons less eternal.

Or perhaps learning may be itself an environment, a different place that is neither a natural occurrence, nor a routine or artificial place, but a specially constructed opening, or threshold of mind that by its nature tends to urge us forward, to create important moments. Think of what we learn in hospitals or churches, hospices or retreats, think of our awarenesses there. These are places for solitude and meditation, or situations where choices and values are required; where tensions must be resolved by reflection and action; where hypotheses and hopes must be explored and modified; where faith and belief may be tested, affirmed, or disconfirmed; where we are either sustained or abandoned by what we understand. Perhaps this is learning.

My approach to understanding the invisible work of adult learning has for decades been invested in the idea that adults constantly challenge themselves with the continuing unfinished issues, unfinished events, in their lives. These forms of work are invisible because they are often unarticulated and perhaps they lie beyond conscious words. Yet they are immensely real and practical: how to construct something, how to earn a livelihood, how to care well for another, how to develop a skill or an art, how to solve a troubled relationship or find meaning in a bleak landscape. How much in any one life is incomplete in this way? We often have to learn how to nourish such incomplete, unfinished issues.

Living with unfinished issues is the adult situation that leads toward learning and requires us to assert our individual form of integrity. The unfinished issue leads a learner toward tools, resources, institutions, and more experienced, more knowing, other human beings. The carefully crafted question is an engine of meaning; in its construction, language, and precision, it carries the inquirer forward.

If the question is good enough, its logic and language, the implied dimensions of the unknown, and its apparent context all assist usefully in the construction of a fitting response. Yet sometimes the best learning happens because a question has such richness that it nurtures and sustains new discourse about possibilities, new interpretations of the shape and power of what we have not yet understood.

Perhaps this is learning, an accurate and satisfying interpretation of the possibilities surrounding an unknown. This idea holds the implication that learning has a future, that it remains (in Abraham Kaplan's words) "dynamically open,"[3] and will be (in Karl Popper's words) "tentative for ever."[5] Perhaps it is our openness to new events, perhaps this is learning.

"Possibilities" also leads to Jerome Bruner, who says that learning involves "going beyond the information given"—that is, taking what information we have and reorganizing, recombining, and reconnecting it in such a way that new possibilities of understanding and insight appear.[6] This means that, in the information we are given and the information we encounter through our own powers of discovery, we learn by finding and sorting consistencies from chaos.

When new groups gather and engage in conversations, for example when we come together as a class or a conference, or as a family reunion, we present ourselves and cautiously learn who we are by seeking patterns and connections in our experiences, and by discovering shared or contrasting values. If we are lucky, perhaps this permits the new learning of a good conversation to occur.

If learning is the admission of the possible to our thinking, it means that we must learn to construct new contexts—we might call them transitional zones—where unusual and perhaps unexpected knowledge can be temporarily organized. This cognitive garden might offer a fine metaphor for comprehending the unexpected as we encounter it: a little snake among the asters, a hummingbird at the hollyhocks. It might be a useful metaphor to understand our learning events, like conversations and reading, as ways that require us to enter the gardens of other learners to see how they are organized, and what they grow, and if they have some seeds. When we exchange ideas in these places, we might experience the most stimulating device for learning, *surprise*—especially surprise that touches our interests and unknowns. Perhaps this is learning: the best learners live up to these surprises and pursue them more fearlessly than others.

If I were to offer a credo for learning as I see it, it would have several tenets, none immutable, all tentative.

For me, learning requires the face-to-face presence of other learners whose experiences and stories inspire the models of thought and possibility we require if we are to learn how to interpret our own moments of surprise.

Learning should be a profoundly social event, as well as a surprising one. If we are to help, the process ought to have a human being visible to us.

The situation for learning requires time and a process; it slowly fosters adaptation. Without reflective, critical thought, learning will not happen. Instant access to information does not assist the learner toward coherence in leading one life; it may, in fact, contribute to entropy and chaos, situations where no one learns anything. We can read anything, perhaps, but only one text at a time. Perhaps learning requires slow information; perhaps this is the more valuable, more human thing. When we slow the process, we also allow more things to happen, and more discoveries to occur.

For me, among all the cognitive possibilities essential to the learner, there must be an exquisite sense that *learning is possible, it is a natural and personal thing to do.* At times we often need others who can say to us with authority and trust, *Here are the possibilities for you as I see them.*

To be responsible to learners, to design situations where they will encounter their own possibilities, we need to be in situations where individuals can come to understand their own perceived needs for resolution and change. This may be a fear that needs to be made smaller, a skill or a new perspective to be mastered, or an articulate hypothesis ready for exploration. But learners need to speak it, they need to identify the unknown, they need to describe the events that need to happen, in words of their own.

Every human being is an incomplete, impermanent artifact of aspirations and experiences, sustaining in one life the cumulative traces of engagement, reflection, possibility, loss, and challenge that accrue over a lifetime. These traces make us different. Every person who strives—each of us—finds the world to be incomplete, unfinished in a slightly different way.

Each of us is unfinished differently from all others, and—no matter how far we have come from our youth, no matter how well traveled and deeply experienced we are—we are continuously capable of new questions, new lessons, and new experiences, many started long ago. Cultural institutions should think of themselves thriving on the discovery in every life of these new possibilities.

Like our handmade lives and private differences, every library volume and museum object shows the traces of a person's engagement with skill, passion, and mystery. We can see how the book or the painting was intended to fill the incompleteness of the world and overcome human impermanence in it. Still, like the artist, we know that nothing we make or understand will stop our disappearing.

Disappearing as we are, there are mysteries to admire: these books and artifacts never yield fully to our presence or to our asking, although we strive to know something beyond their evidence and their origins. These mysteries will outlast us, because we are no more permanent in life as a consequence of what we have made, what we have seen, or what we have said. The objects we love and their unknowns will remain, and we cannot. We leave.

And yet: our lives are not immutable or predetermined; and we are made more memorable because we have left a trace of our own design. We are ourselves less mysterious because we have crafted and expressed our truths as well as we can. We are less alone because we have stood among other lives, saying things.

Perhaps this is learning. Among objects of belief and objects of doubt alike, among ideas of the past and ideas of the future, we strive to feel in some way continuous with the traces that mark other lives, while we also confirm the solitary uniqueness of our own. We go to libraries, we go to museums. We want to understand the sources and consequences of belief and hope, of believing and hoping and moving forward as more whole human beings. We inquire because it is a part of what we are.

We hope for a journey beyond the usual dimensions of experience. We believe that we are capable of understanding more; that we will understand more. We reflect on the meanings of possible but unproven relationships with other human beings, with cultures we can never visit, with an invisible divinity or an imperceptible pattern in the world as we know it. What if? We are enchanted by hypothesis: we test, we test, we test. Perhaps this is learning.

Our actions, our traces, our lives, our relationships, we come to see, are meant to express promises and attempt to fulfill them by being open and slow to assume anything, by judging only when the evidence is complete. Reflections on knowledge and immersions in the evidence most worthy of trust will help us to overcome the fractures and divisions of the world. By saying our promises to each other and our aspirations for our own learning, we act to make the invisible present; we immerse ourselves in the possible.

In each person these reflections, these traces of what we might come to understand against the odds, are at first invisible, and even as we see them emerge slowly and take form, we do not know what they (and we) might still become. We are capable and constructive, though we may neither weave nor build. Still, we can find many ways to defeat our own potential for isolation and despair. We might rescue each other when we stand together, when we read and look and speak. We might rescue ourselves. Perhaps this is learning.

NOTES

1. Gordon Allport, *Becoming: Basic Considerations for a Psychology of Personality* (New Haven: Yale University Press, 1955).

2. Eduard Lindeman, *The Meaning of Adult Education* (New York: New Republic, 1926).

3. John W. Gardner, *Self-Renewal: The Individual and the Innovative Society* (New York: Harper & Row, 1964).

4. Abraham Kaplan, *The Conduct of Inquiry: Methodology for Behavioral Science* (San Francisco: Chandler Publishing, 1964), 68–71.

5. Karl R. Popper, *The Logic of Scientific Discovery* (New York: Science Editions, 1961), 280–281.

6. Jerome Bruner, *Beyond the Information Given: Studies in the Psychology of Knowing* (New York: Norton, 1973), 218–238.

INDEX

ABOUT THE AUTHOR

David Carr is a member of the faculty at the University of North Carolina at Chapel Hill, where he teaches librarianship. He has been an educator, consultant, and advocate for critical thinking and reflective practice in cultural institutions for more than thirty-five years. His collection of essays, *The Promise of Cultural Institutions*, was published by AltaMira Press in 2003.